Compton Verney Handbook

Published 2004 by Compton Verney House Trust
© Compton Verney House Trust

ISBN 0-9546545-1-X

Designed by Anne Odling-Smee/O-SB
Proof-read by Annelise Hone and Alex Stetter
Copy-edited by Paul Holberton
Production co-ordinated by Uwe Kraus
Printed in Italy

With special thanks for their contributions to Charles Beddington,
Norbert Jopek and Professor Dame Jessica Rawson.

With thanks for their assistance to Diane Bilbey, Dr Steven Brindle,
Dr Matthew Eve, Antonia Harrison, Professor Riccardo Lattuada, John Leslie,
Dr James Lin, Richard Lockett, Dr Sylvia Pinches, Katia Pisvin, Dr Wang Tao.

Cover image: the west front of Compton Verney with the new extension
completed in 1998; inside cover: adapted from a design by Robert Adam for
the ceiling of the Hall at Compton Verney, 1763, pencil, pen and ink.

Notes: an asterisk in the text denotes an entry in the glossary on page 188.
Naples, German and British collections: all paintings are painting size
unless otherwise stated. British Folk Art and Marx-Lambert Collections:
all paintings are framed size unless otherwise stated.

Compton Verney House Trust was founded by Sir Peter Moores
and is funded by the Peter Moores Foundation

Compton Verney Handbook

Compiled by Dr Susan Jenkins

Selected works

Contents

The House and Grounds

The first record of a settlement at the site now called Compton Verney was the late Saxon village of Compton ('cumb' = valley, 'tun' = farm: 'farm in the valley'). It had good communication, being served by the Roman road, the Fosse Way, which ran north-south half a mile from the site and led to the Roman settlements of Cirencester and Leicester. By the time of the Domesday Book in 1086 (a survey ordered by the Norman king, William the Conqueror, to record land tenure and values), the village was divided into two manors. The largest manor was held by the Count of Meulan, from whom it descended to the earls of Warwick, who remained overlords, subject to the king.

Some time before 1150, the manor was granted by the Earl of Warwick to Robert Murdak and the village became known as Compton Murdak, passing by inheritance to the heirs of the Murdak family. In 1370, after two hundred years of Murdak ownership, Sir Thomas Murdak handed over the estate to Edward III's mistress, Alice Perrers. The Verney family had begun acquiring lands in the area of Compton Murdak and the surrounding villages before purchasing the estate, which in 1435 was acquired by the ambitious Richard Verney (died 1490) with the assistance of his younger brother, John Verney, Dean of Lichfield, and of the Earl of Warwick, the powerful Richard Beauchamp, Verney's employer.

By about 1500 Compton Murdak was so closely associated with the Verney family that it began to be known as Compton Verney. Richard Verney also built a manor-house there in about 1442, as recorded in William Dugdale's *Antiquities of Warwickshire* (1656):

Richard Verney Esquire (afterward Knight) ... built a great part of the House, as it now standeth, wherein,

A watercolour set in a roundel on a wall panel at Compton Verney, depicting the house and lake about 1830.

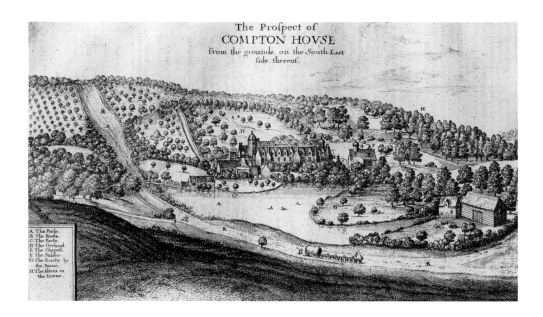

The Prospect of
COMPTON HOVSE
from the grounds, on the South East
side thereof.

A. The Poole.
B. The Roade.
C. The Parke.
D. The Orchard.
E. The Chappell.
F. The Stables.
G. The Banke by
the Barne.
H. The Elmes in
the Towne.

*besides his own Armes with matches, he then set up …
towards the upper end of the Hall, the Armes of King
Henry the Sixth.*[1]

The house was further extended in the period 1500–
1650, probably after the marriage of another Richard
Verney (dates of tenure at Compton Verney 1574–1630)
to Margaret, daughter of Sir Fulke Greville of Beauchamps
Court, Alcester, a wealthy heiress with claims to the
dormant barony of Willoughby de Broke

Very little is known about this early house at Compton
Verney, but a drawing by Wenceslaus Hollar, dated about
1655, which was published by William Dugdale, shows a
great hall and a long south wing looking down to the lake,
with gabled dormer* windows and chimneys with octagonal
turrets at either end, also kitchens to the left (south-west)
and a chapel (figure 1). The first surviving inventory of the

1. 'The Prospect of Compton
House', engraving after a
drawing by Wenceslaus
Hollar dated about 1655,
published in William
Dugdale's *Antiquities of
Warwickshire* in 1656.
A. The Poole
B. The Roade
C. The Parke
D. The Orchard
E. The Chappell
F. The Stables
G. The Banke by the Barne
H. The Elmes in the Towne

house, dating from the Civil War (1642), describes a house of thirty rooms, including a hall (Great Chamber), two parlours, seventeen bedrooms, an armoury and a study, as well as servants' quarters and outbuildings; these were furnished with velvet, tapestry and pictures to a total value of £900. A silk-and-wool embroidery depicting Lucretia's Banquet (figure 2), which was sold from Compton Verney in 1913 to the Victoria and Albert Museum in London, may have been one of the original pieces hanging in the Great Chamber at this period.

Until now, the Verneys had not pursued their claim to the title of barons Willoughby de Broke. However, when Richard Verney (1622–1711) inherited the estate in 1683, following the failure of the direct male line after ten generations, he decided to exert his claim to the barony. In 1696 the House of Lords accepted the claim and Richard Verney became 11th Baron Willoughby de Broke, de jure.*

Richard Verney's son, George, 12th Baron Willoughby de Broke, inherited the estate in 1711 (tenure at Compton

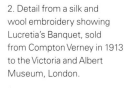

2. Detail from a silk and wool embroidery showing Lucretia's Banquet, sold from Compton Verney in 1913 to the Victoria and Albert Museum, London.

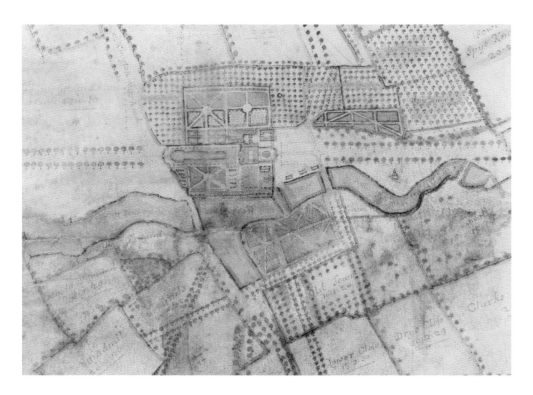

Verney 1711–28). This was a period when medieval houses such as the Duke of Devonshire's Chatsworth House were being remodelled and new country seats such as the Duke of Marlborough's Blenheim Palace in nearby Woodstock were being built. George, 12th Baron commissioned an extensive reconstruction of the earlier house, whilst preserving much of the plan of the original building. There is no evidence concerning his choice of architect, although the names of Sir John Vanbrugh (employed at Blenheim Palace) and Francis Smith of Warwick have been associated with the project. Since John, 14th Baron would soon remodel the house in his turn, it is difficult to know exactly what George, 12th Baron's house looked like. A map of the site of around

3. Compton Verney, the house and grounds, from an estate map by James Fish of 1736.

1736 shows that it was a square block with the stables to the north (still existing, built by the Scottish architect James Gibbs in about 1735), with formal gardens to the north and south and the main approach to the house running east to west, with an ornamental canal running beside the west lawn (figure 3). South of the lake was an area of plantations crossed by avenues. A visitor, John Loveday of Caversham, described the house in 1735:

> *Just on the right of the road between Little Keinton and Wellsburn is the seat of the Hon. Mr Verney …*
> *It stands low and is built of Stone; the front is towards the Garden and has 11 Windows … Below there is an handsome Gallery or Dancing Room … The Gardens, with the room taken up by the house contain 20 Acres. The Gardens rise up an hill, and are well-contrived for Use and Convenience. There are Views down to a Pond; of these Ponds there are 4 in a string, which make a mile in length.*[2]

On the 1736 map there are in fact five ponds, although one of these is marked 'new pool'.

The surviving evidence, which includes two inventories dating from the period, indicates that George, 12th Baron had built a courtyard house, entered from the east as it is now, through an archway with a cupola* in the now-lost east range. The main apartments were in the west and south wings, with the servants' quarters on the north side. The west range was dominated by the Great Hall, which probably occupied the same site as the original medieval Great Chamber. The Great Staircase led up from the Hall to the main apartments above.

George, 12th Baron had thus remodelled the house and gardens to create an estate suitable for a family with what was effectively a new title. After he and both his sons died, his great-nephew, John Peyto Verney (tenure 1741–1816) became 14th Baron and also inherited the neighbouring estate of Chesterton, raising the household's income to about £4,000 a year. This additional income and his marriage in 1761 to the sister of Lord North (from nearby Wroxton Abbey, Oxfordshire) may have encouraged him to improve the estate and remodel the house and grounds once again.

In 1760 he commissioned the rising Scottish architect, Robert Adam, to propose alterations to Compton Verney. Adam's projected remodelling went further than anything that had taken place before. His drawings of the ground, first and attic storeys (figure 4) show what was to be retained from the original building and what was to be demolished.[3] Three of the four sides of the original court-yard house (the east, north and south wings) were to be

4. Robert Adam's plan of the ground floor of the house showing proposed new work in darker shading, dated about 1760, pencil, pen and ink with colour washes.

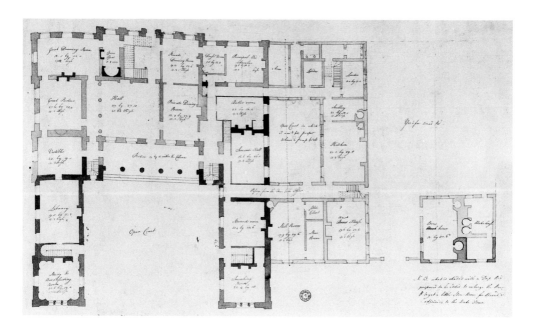

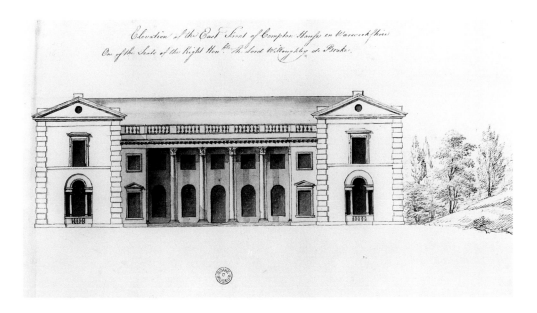

Elevation of the East Front of Compton House in Warwickshire
One of the Seats of the Right Honble. R. Lord Willoughby de Broke.

5. Robert Adam's design for the east front at Compton Verney, 1760, pencil, pen and ink with grey wash.

torn down, and Adam proposed the addition of a portico* on the new east front and the rebuilding of the north and south wings, to give the house its present U-shape.

The building work was carried out from about 1762 to 1768, supervised by the Warwick architect and mason, William Hiorn, who was also employed locally at Charlecote Park and Stoneleigh Abbey. The stone came from the estate and the local quarries of Warwick, Hornton, Gloucester and Painswick. The most important changes that Adam made included the removal of the Great Staircase on the west front and its replacement by a Saloon with columns in pairs, alterations to the Hall, and the creation of an attic storey above it. Adam also added a library and octagonal study to the south wing and adapted the brewhouse and bakery to the north of the house. The floor plans of the house were published in 1771 in the fifth volume of the survey of Britain's great

6. The Hall at Compton
Verney, 1913 (*Country Life*
18 October 1913, p. 534).

houses, *Vitruvius Britannicus*,* which shows certain
differences from Adam's drawings, suggesting that some
of the Baroque interiors had been left as they were.

Robert Adam was often responsible for the interior
decoration as well as the architectural design of his
buildings; however, at Compton Verney, he designed the
decoration of only a few rooms, including the Hall and the
Saloon – the remainder of the house was decorated by
local craftsmen using their own pattern-book* designs.
There is an undated drawing in the Victoria and Albert
Museum for the decoration of the Hall showing three
large plaster picture-frames, placed high on the walls. Two
of these can be seen in a photograph published in *Country
Life* magazine in 1913, containing the large landscape
paintings with classical ruins that were painted for this

location (figure 6). The paintings were executed by the Venetian artist Antonio Zucchi (1726–1795), who frequently worked with Robert Adam, and were removed from the house after its sale by the Verney family in 1921.

It is this period in the history of the house that is captured in the painting by the German immigrant artist Johann Zoffany, now in the J. Paul Getty Museum in Los Angeles (figure 7). The painting, which is dated about 1766, shows John, 14th Baron and his family preparing to take tea, possibly in the Breakfast Room at Compton Verney.

Building work continued on the lesser buildings at Compton Verney until the 1780s, and during this period

7. *A Group Portrait of John, 14th Lord Willoughby de Broke, and his family in the Breakfast Room at Compton Verney,* by Johann Zoffany, about 1766, oil on canvas, J. Paul Getty Museum, Los Angeles.

the grounds were also re-landscaped. In 1769–70,
for instance, the Green House (which no longer survives)
was constructed, and in 1771–2 the ice-house and 'Cow
House' were finished.

In 1769, soon after Robert Adam's architectural
work was completed, the celebrated landscape architect
Lancelot 'Capability' Brown was employed to re-landscape
the grounds in keeping with the new taste for idealised
nature in garden design. He removed all traces of the
earlier formal gardens, including the canal on the west
front and the avenues running east to west, replacing them
with lawns and trees, planting clumps of cedars and over
2,200 oak and ash saplings. He also turned the lakes into
a single expanse of water by removing the dam between
the Upper Long Pool and the Middle Pool to make way for
his Upper Bridge, and in 1772 demolished the old chapel
between the house and the lake. He had built a new
chapel, on the slope to the north of the house, earlier, in
1766–8, although works were not completed there until
1780, for a total cost of £981 10s 4d. The tombs of earlier
Verneys were moved to the new chapel, along with a
mixture of English and German stained glass which had
decorated the old chapel (figure 8). The tombs can still be
seen in situ*, but the glass was unfortunately sold and
dispersed in the twentieth century.

In the years following the death in 1816 of John, 14th
Baron, remembered as 'the good Lord Willoughby', there
were minor alterations to the building: for instance, the
architect Henry Hakewill transformed the Saloon into a
Dining Room in 1824 for the solitary 16th Baron, Henry
Peyto Verney (tenure 1816–62), before his marriage in
1829, and John Gibson made changes to the Hall, including
the addition of the hunting frieze, in about 1863 for Henry,
18th Baron (tenure 1862–1902). There was also minor work

8. Detail from a stained glass
window originally in the chapel
at Compton Verney, now in
Warwick Museum, showing
Anne, Lady Verney, with her
five daughters, about 1520.

in the grounds, including the extension of the lower lake by the engineer William Whitmore in about 1815 and the erection of an obelisk (a miniature copy of the obelisk outside the Lateran Church* in Rome) over the old family vault near the lake in about 1848, which can still be seen.

Since that time, the history of the estate has been a chequered one. Compton Verney suffered in the agricultural depression of the 1870s and 1880s, in common with landed estates across the country, and the house was let out from 1887. The last Verney to live at Compton Verney was Richard Greville Verney, 19th Baron (tenure 1902–21), whose nostalgic memoir, *The Passing Years*, offers a sentimental description of life in the house before he was obliged to sell it in 1921 (he died two years later, in 1923).

The next seventy years in the history of the estate were troubled, and it changed hands a number of times. The new owner in 1921 was Joseph Watson, Lord Manton, a soap manufacturer and racehorse owner, created Baron Manton of Compton Verney in 1922, a few months before

9. Peter Hall directing Shakespeare's *A Midsummer Night's Dream* with Judy Dench as Titania and Ian Richardson as Oberon, in the grounds of Compton Verney, 1969.

10. Aerial photograph of Compton Verney featuring a project by artist Anya Gallaccio, inspired by Robert Adam's design for the ceiling of the Hall, 2000.

1. Quote from William Dugdale: *Antiquities of Warwickshire*, London, 1656, p. 435, new edition edited by W. Thomas, 2 volumes, London, 1730, volume I, p. 565.
2. S. Markham, *John Loveday of Caversham*, Salisbury 1984, p.190.
3. One of Adam's drawings for the elevation of the east front of the house, dated 2 September 1760, is at Sir John Soane's Museum in London (Adam Drawings, volume 41, number 17).

he died. His son sold the estate in 1929 to Samuel Lamb and his family, who moved out in World War II when the house was requisitioned by the army and the grounds were used as an experimental station for smoke-screen camouflage. The house was never lived in again. In 1958 it was acquired by the bachelor Harry Ellard, who occasionally authorised film companies to shoot in the grounds (figure 9). By the 1980s it had become semi-derelict. In 1993 it was purchased by the Peter Moores Foundation, which set up the Compton Verney House Trust. An extensive building programme has given it a new life as an art gallery, enabling it to open its doors and welcome visitors once again (figure 10).

List of owners of Compton Verney, with dates of tenure:

John Verney, died 1457
Richard Verney, 1435–1490
Edmund Verney, 1490–1495
Richard Verney, 1495–1526
Thomas Verney, 1526–1557
Richard Verney, 1557–1567
George Verney, 1567–1574
Richard Verney, 1574–1630
Greville Verney, 1630–1642
Greville Verney, 1642–1648
Greville Verney, 1649–1668
William Verney, 1668–1683
Richard Verney, 11th Baron Willoughby de Broke, 1683–1711
George Verney, 12th Baron, 1711–1728
[Richard Verney, 13th Baron, 1693–1752, never owned the estate]
John Verney, 1728–1741
John Peyto Verney, 14th Baron, 1741–1816
[John Verney, 15th Baron, 1762–1820, was insane and never took possession]
Henry Peyto Verney, 16th Baron, 1816–1852
Robert John (Barnard) Verney, 17th Baron, 1852–1862
Henry Verney, 18th Baron, 1862–1902
Richard Greville Verney, 19th Baron, 1902–1921
Joseph Watson, Lord Manton and son, 1921–1929
Mr Morgan, Mr Wilson and 2nd Lord Manton, 1929–1933
Samuel Lamb, 1933–1958
Harry Ellard, 1958–1983
Period and Country Houses Ltd, 1983–1993
Peter Moores Foundation (for the Compton Verney House Trust) 1993–

The south front of
Compton Verney with the
lake and grounds.

The Collection

The six collections on view at Compton Verney reflect
the interests of its founder, Sir Peter Moores, and
highlight areas that are under-represented in galleries in
the United Kingdom. The collection of fine and decorative
art from Naples, in Southern Italy, represents its 'Golden
Age' from 1600 to 1800, and includes works by artists
such as Luca Giordano, Francesco Solimena and Pietro
Fabris. The collection of late medieval art from Germany
in the period 1450–1650 features wooden sculptures and
panel paintings that originally decorated church altars.
There is also a small collection of British portraits, and
a unique collection of British folk art together with the
Marx-Lambert collection (formed by the textile and graphic
designer Enid Marx and her friend Margaret Lambert).
The collection of objects from China consists mainly of
bronzes used in burial rituals. It is perhaps one of the best
collections of Chinese bronzes in the United Kingdom
after that in the British Museum.

Detail from a pair of tables
(South Italian or Spanish).
See page 63.

Naples 1600–1800

Bernardo Strozzi (1581–1644)
The Incredulity of Saint Thomas, 1620s
Oil on canvas, 89 × 98.2 cm

Bernardo Strozzi, the greatest Genoese artist
of his time, painted at least two other versions
of the scene depicted here. The Apostle Thomas,
who had doubted Christ's return from the dead,
is seen here taking up Christ's invitation to insert
his fingers into the wounds in His side caused
at His crucifixion by the Centurion's spear, in order
to confirm His identity. This is one of Strozzi's
most powerful paintings, in which the delicate
handling of Jesus' body contrasts with the rough
and stooping appearance of the inquisitive Saint
Thomas. Almost certainly inspired by an earlier
painting by Caravaggio of the same subject
(painted in 1602–3), Strozzi's more elegant work
may also have been influenced by the style of
the Flemish artist Anthony Van Dyck, who was
working in Genoa at the invitation of the Genoese
aristocracy during this period .

Previous page: Detail from Pierre-
Jacques Volaire's *An Eruption of
Vesuvius by Moonlight'*, see page 53.

Bernardo Cavallino (1616–1656)
The Flight into Egypt, about 1640–50
Oil on canvas, 76.8 × 63.5 cm

The Flight into Egypt is briefly narrated by Saint Matthew in the second chapter of his Gospel: warned by an angel that King Herod had ordered all infants in Bethlehem to be killed, Joseph "rose and took the child and his mother by night, and departed into Egypt". Following the biblical account, Cavallino represents the scene at nightfall, in a dense wood. Mary sits on a tired donkey and appears to be handing some fruit to Jesus who is resting in her lap, while Joseph can just be made out in the background. The predominantly sombre tones of the painting emphasise the hasty and secret nature of the flight, and it is only a narrow shaft of light which illuminates the focal point of the painting, the melancholy group of the Mother and Child.

Such paintings, in a dark tonality that contrasts with the area of strong light, were made popular by Caravaggio in the 1590s and in Naples remained fashionable until the 1650s. The Neapolitan Bernardo Cavallino probably trained with Massimo Stanzione, who was well known for this type of work.

Francesco Solimena (1657–1747)
Venus with lapis tending the Wounded Aeneas
(top); *Priam, King of Troy, begging Achilles for the
Body of Hector*, about 1695
Both paintings oil on canvas, 48.9 × 100.3 cm

These two sketches, known in Italian as *bozzetti*
or *modelli*, are designs for two larger canvases, one
of which, *Venus with lapis tending the Wounded
Aeneas*, is also in the collection at Compton Verney
(see page 32). It was common practice for artists to
make preparatory drawings and oil sketches to work
out their compositions, and to show to possible
purchasers. As a painter of historical scenes
Francesco Solimena also used this working method.

    The subjects of both paintings are taken from
classical epic poems. The scene showing Priam,
King of Troy, comes from Homer's *Iliad*, in which Priam
begs Achilles to accept a ransom for the body of
his son Hector, whom Achilles has killed. The scene
with Venus and lapis is taken from Virgil's *Aeneid*.
Venus, Aeneas's mother, has come to his rescue with
medicinal herbs with which lapis may make a potion
to dislodge the arrow stuck in Aeneas's leg. The sketch
is very similar in composition to the much larger
finished painting.

Francesco Solimena (1657–1747)
Venus with lapis tending the Wounded Aeneas,
about 1695
Oil on canvas, 210.8 × 365.8 cm

Francesco Solimena was the most important
Neapolitan artist of his generation. This impressive
canvas shows a scene from Virgil's *Aeneid*, in which
Aeneas's mother, Venus (descending on a cloud)
brings lapis, who tends him, the herbs he needs
to heal the wound in his leg. It is a magnificent
example of the kind of heroic scene from history
with which the public areas of Italian palaces were
adorned in the Baroque era. Such works were often
paired across the room, and this one was probably
accompanied by a pendant* of *Priam, King of Troy,
begging Achilles for the Body of Hector*, now lost.
Sketches for both these canvases are also in the
Compton Verney collection (see page 30).

Luca Forte (about 1615 – before 1670)
Still Life with Apples, Grapes and a Dragonfly
Signed *l.f.*
Oil on copper, 15.6 × 20.6 cm

Luca Forte was one of the pioneers of still-life
painting in Naples – especially of fruit – which was
an important genre of painting there. It emerged
in Naples as a genre in its own right around 1600
and flourished from about the mid-1620s. Although
Luca Forte signed his works, he never dated them,
and little is known about his life. It can only be
assumed that he was active mainly in the period
1620–50. This unusual still-life composition was
painted on copper, a support favoured by artists for
small-scale works. The smooth and uniform surface
of copper allowed the use of a very fine brush to
bring small details, such as the dragonfly hovering
above the bunch of grapes in this work, into focus,
and enabled the artist to bring out the polished
surfaces of fruits, as here.

Paolo Porpora (1617–1675)

*Still Life with Flowers in an Urn, Butterflies
and a Snake*

Oil on canvas, 129 × 98.5 cm

Paolo Porpora was born in Naples and at the age
of fifteen entered the studio of Giacomo Recco,
who, with Luca Forte, was one of the earliest
exponents of Neapolitan flower painting. In 1650
Porpora moved to Rome, where he worked for
the powerful Chigi family. The majority of his
still lifes, however, were produced in Naples.
Bernardo de Dominici, the biographer of the
Neapolitan artists of the period, praised Porpora's
accomplishments in terms which do justice to
this sparkling and exquisitely detailed flower
composition: "… leaving behind that dry mode
of composition [of Luca Forte], [Porpora] began
to make a copious arrangement of delightful
inventions … his paintings were a marvellous
example of their kind".

Giuseppe Ruoppolo (died 1710)
Still Life with Fruit and Mushrooms
Signed: *G.R....polo*
Oil on canvas, 75 × 101 cm

Giuseppe Ruoppolo belonged to one of the
leading families of still-life painters in Naples.
He was the nephew of Giovan Battista Ruoppolo,
who was renowned for his splendid compositions
of fruit and had many followers besides his nephew
(see page 40). Neapolitan still life developed in
parallel with the Netherlandish tradition of still life;
although its stylistic sources have been debated,
it was clearly influenced by the work of Caravaggio,
who was active in Naples, and was not simply a
response to northern art. Neapolitan artists such
as Giuseppe Ruoppolo were able to evolve a
distinctive native style of still life.

Giovan Battista Ruoppolo (1629–1693)
Still Life of Figs, Cherries, Plums and other Fruit,
with two Guinea Pigs (top); *Still Life of Watermelons,*
Plums, Cherries, Figs, Pears and a Monkey
Oil on canvas, 57.8 × 133 cm and 57.8 × 131.7 cm

Giovan Battista Ruoppolo was one of the most
sought-after painters of still life in Naples. His
pictures were collected by the aristocracy and
the mercantile élite, and this pair of fruit still lifes,
with their long rectangular format, was probably
designed to be hung over interior doors in a *palazzo*.
The landscape background of the composition with
two guinea pigs, happily feeding on cherries and
plums, is a typical Neapolitan invention; Mount
Vesuvius, which overlooks the town, can just be
made out on the left. In both compositions the
fruits, displayed on a ledge, are subtly lit. In one,
a monkey peers out from behind half a watermelon,
having just gnawed away the melon beside him,
ready to start on the basket of figs.

Gaspar van Wittel, called Gaspare Vanvitelli (1652/3–1736)
A View of Posillipo with the Palazzo Donn' Anna,
about 1700–1
Oil on canvas, 72.7 × 170.3 cm

Van Wittel's stay in Naples (1699–1702) was prompted by the invitation of the Spanish Viceroy, Don Luis de la Cerda, Duke of Medinaceli. The Duke was a great enthusiast of the artist's work and commissioned over thirty paintings from him. Van Wittel specialised in the type of views known in Italian as *veduta esatta* or accurate view, and indeed a large number of buildings on the Bay of Naples are identifiable in this painting. They include the Palazzo Donn' Anna, in the left foreground, which may have been occupied by the Viceroy. The gondolas crossing the bay are carrying aristocratic passengers, possibly the Viceroy's entourage. Resembling Venetian gondolas, they were probably introduced by the artist to add a note of contrasting colour to this predominantly light-blue composition. In 1701, Don Luis returned to Spain, taking his views of Naples with him as souvenirs. This painting remained in his family until it was acquired for Compton Verney in 2001.

Gaspar van Wittel, called Gaspare Vanvitelli (1652/3–1736)

The Grotto of Pozzuoli, Naples, with Virgil's Tomb, 1702
Signed and dated *GAS V W/ 1702*
Oil on canvas, 49 × 64.2 cm

The Dutch artist Gaspar van Wittel settled in Rome
in 1674 and became one of the leading painters
of the topographical* views of Italy so popular
with foreign visitors. From 1699 to 1702 he lived
in Naples, whence this view originates. The Grotto
of Pozzuoli was a favourite tourist destination
thanks to its classical associations. The grotto,
which is in fact a tunnel, was built by the Roman
Emperor Coccius Nerva, while the domed structure
above and to the left of its entrance was believed
to be the tomb of the great classical poet Virgil.
Van Wittel has animated the view with a variety
of local figures, including a beggar, a pair of friars
and a man on horseback. He produced over
twelve versions of this attractive canvas in order
to satisfy demand.

Francesco de Mura (1696–1782)
Saint Nicholas of Bari received into Paradise, 1733–4
Oil on canvas, 139 × 224 cm

Francesco de Mura trained in the studio of the
great Neapolitan painter Francesco Solimena and
was one of the leading fresco* painters in Naples
from the 1730s. This painting is a highly finished
sketch (or *modello*), which may have been painted
to show the patron the proposed appearance of
the finished composition or to guide the artist's
assistants in the execution of the initial stages.
The commission was to decorate the interior of
the dome in the church of San Nicola alla Carità in
Naples, where De Mura's fresco survives, but in
poor condition. The busy composition, which would
have wrapped around the dome of the church,
shows Christ with God the Father and the dove
of the Holy Ghost (the Holy Trinity) welcoming
Saint Nicholas into Paradise. Saint Nicholas, who
was a bishop in what is now Turkey, around 400 AD,
is shown dressed in orange vestments, with a
cherub holding his crozier,* lower centre left. Shortly
before 1100 AD his relics were removed to Bari,
on the east coast of Italy. He was celebrated for
rescuing sailors and for bringing gifts to the poor,
providing the basis for the story of Santa Claus.

Giuseppe Bonito (1707–1789)
The Poet (top); *The Music Lesson*, about 1742
Both paintings oil on canvas, 101.5 × 154 cm

Like Francesco de Mura, Giuseppe Bonito studied
with the influential Neapolitan artist Francesco
Solimena. He became court painter to the King of
Naples in 1751, and in 1755 head of the Academy
of Drawing and of the tapestry manufacturers in
Naples. He is now admired above all for his popular
everyday-life or 'genre' scenes such as these two
paintings. This pair of canvases, which was only
recently reunited, was once part of a set of four
that were sent to Spain in Bonito's lifetime (the
other two showed girls sewing and boys reading).
The paintings would have represented a cross-
section of life in Naples. *The Poet* is a smiling,
bohemian figure in an unbuttoned shirt surrounded
by admiring patrons, one of whom engages the
viewer with a sidelong glance. The nobleman and
the beautiful pianist in *The Music Lesson* wear rich,
elegant clothing, whilst in the background on the
right the servants are painted in simpler garments.

Carlo Bonavia (1751–1788)
A Storm off a Rocky Coast, 1757
Signed and dated lower left *Bonavia P.A. 1757*
Oil on canvas, 126.5 × 207 cm

This painting depicts a dramatic shipwreck,
with figures in the foreground struggling to save
possessions and lives. The crew and cargo being
rescued were probably on a ship bound for Naples,
as the trunk being pulled ashore bears the name of
this destination. Members of the crew can be seen
swimming towards the shore, grasping the rocks,
being pulled by rope from the sea and being revived
on land. Although this is almost certainly not an
'exact' topographical* view, it recalls rocky coasts
near Naples. Bonavia's style may be seen as an
Italian variant of that of Claude-Joseph Vernet,
the foremost French painter of marine scenes of
the eighteenth century. Vernet lived in Rome from
1734 until 1735 and visited Naples in 1737 and
1746. Bonavia may have been of Roman origin but
his career was spent entirely in Naples, where he
enjoyed considerable success among foreign
visitors as well as local collectors.

Pierre-Jacques Volaire (1729 – about 1792)

An Eruption of Vesuvius by Moonlight
Signed, dated and inscribed *Eruption du Mont Vésuve … sur le lieu par le Che. Volaire 1774*
Oil on canvas, 130 × 260 cm

Volaire was a native of Toulon, in the south of France, and there met the painter Claude-Joseph Vernet when Vernet was working on his masterpieces, a series of views of the ports of France. Volaire remained Vernet's assistant for eight years before emigrating to Rome in 1764 and subsequently settling in Naples in 1769. There he became famous for his numerous large paintings of Mount Vesuvius, which erupted several times in the 1770s, including 1774, the year of this painting. It was traditional (though dangerous) for tourists to visit the erupting volcano, and Volaire is documented to have conducted a visit to Vesuvius this very same year with an important client, Bergeret de Grandcourt. Sir William Hamilton, British envoy in Naples, was a regular onlooker at volcanic eruptions, and a dedicated student of the volcanic activity of southern Italy. He published his observations on volcanoes in his book *Campi Phlegraei* two years after this painting was executed. Volaire's spectacular canvas was painted to hang as a pair with a view of the Solfatara, a volcanic crater near Pozzuoli.

Pietro Fabris (active 1754–1804)
The Temple of Hera at Paestum
Oil on canvas, 56.6 × 90.5 cm

Pietro Fabris's origins remain mysterious. He called himself "the English painter" and was described by his patron, Sir William Hamilton, as "a native of Great Britain", but his surviving work is wholly Neapolitan in style and subject-matter. This view of the Temple of Hera at Paestum near Salerno, south of Naples, reflects the revival of interest in the exceptionally well-preserved Greek temples there, which became popular tourist attractions from the 1750s. They were painted by Fabris on a number of occasions. In this work he depicts the second and best preserved of the two temples at Paestum dedicated to Hera (Latin Juno), which dates from about 450 BC. Bathed in a warm sunset light, the ruin is romantically portrayed and evokes the classical past with nostalgia.

Pietro Fabris (active 1754–1804)
View of Naples from the West with Peasants Gaming, 1760s?
Oil on canvas, 71.3 × 98.8 cm

Pietro Fabris was a prolific painter of scenes of Neapolitan peasant life. This work shows musicians, card-players and a wine-seller, all figures which regularly appear in his canvases. Glimpsed like a backdrop through the mouth of the cave they occupy is the Bay of Naples with Castel dell'Ovo and Mount Vesuvius in the distance. Fabris painted a number of different versions of this composition, one of which, in the Royal Collection, is signed and dated 1766. He often painted them in pairs or sets, and it is possible that this work originally had a pendant.* Many of Fabris's views of Naples were engraved, and some were personally hand-coloured by the artist to provide illustrations for Sir William Hamilton's study of volcanoes, the *Campi Phlegraei.*

Pietro Fabris (active 1754–1804)
The Festival of the Madonna dell' Arco, Naples, 1777
Signed and dated lower left *Fabris p.1777*
Oil on canvas, 102.6 × 153.7 cm

Pietro Fabris painted this canvas for the British
envoy in Naples, Sir William Hamilton. Now
perhaps best known as the husband of Nelson's
lover, Emma Hamilton, Sir William was a great
collector of paintings and classical antiquities.
A list of his collection made in 1798 indicates that
this painting hung in an anteroom to the gallery
of his house in Naples, Palazzo Sessa. It was
paired with another work by Fabris, showing a
nocturnal banquet at Posillipo. Hamilton and Fabris
collaborated on a number of projects, including
the production by Fabris of plates for Hamilton's
book about volcanic sites entitled *Campi
Phlegraei.* Both men were interested in Neapolitan
costumes and customs, which inspired this
canvas. The festival depicted was held on Easter
Monday at the church of the Madonna dell' Arco
(seen on the right). The sanctuary housed an image
of the Madonna which was believed to have
miraculously saved the shrine from destruction
during the eruption of Vesuvius in 1631.

Lorenzo Vaccaro (1655–1706)

The Four Continents: Asia, Africa, America and Europe, about 1670–90
Marble, 91, 92, 105 and 95 cm high

Lorenzo Vaccaro was the founder of a dynasty of Neapolitan sculptors and painters. He worked in his native Naples as a painter, sculptor, architect and silversmith, becoming famous for his sculpted busts, portraits and monuments. He was friendly with the important artists working in Naples at the time, particularly the painter Francesco Solimena, whose compositions influenced the style and design of Vaccaro's own work.

These marble busts in an assured, flowing style show the Four Continents as female personifications, all adorned with headdresses. Europe (Europa) wears a military helmet, whereas the bare-breasted figure of America wears an Indian feathered headdress. Both Africa and Asia have flowers and grain intertwined in their hair. In 1692, Vaccaro designed another set of busts of the Four Continents in silver for the Viceroy of Naples, Francesco de Benavides, which were sent back to Spain and are now in Toledo Cathedral.

Lorenzo Vaccaro (1655 – 1706)
Saint Michael, about 1700
Silver and gilt bronze, 29 cm high without base

The sculptor, silversmith and stucco artist
Lorenzo Vaccaro designed several altars, statues
and decorations for churches in Naples. He often
produced designs from which silversmiths would
execute the finished work. This small statue of
Saint Michael in silver and gilded bronze is similar
to the *Saint Michael and the Dragon* in the
treasury of the church of San Gennaro in Naples
(the Cappella del Tesoro di San Gennaro). The
Archangel Michael, whose wings distinguish
him from that other dragon-slayer, Saint George,
wears the armour of a Roman
centurion. He is portrayed with his
traditional spear and shield, here
inscribed with the words *Quis Ut
Deus*, which may mean, 'Who
[would think himself to be] as God?',
referring to Lucifer, who challenged the
Almighty in this way. The Archangel is shown
about to defeat the diminutive figure of the devil
prostrated at his feet.

Maker unknown (South Italian)
Casket, about 1700–50
Inlaid coral and mother-of-pearl, 20.2 × 56.5 × 44 cm

The casket would have contained letters or jewels. It is decorated with many different semi-precious stones, including jasper, agate, lapis lazuli* and moss agate. The stones are held within gilt-brass mounts, which are delicately engraved to resemble leaves. Carved mother-of-pearl and red coral leaves are attached by fine wire all over the box, and its edges are veneered with tortoiseshell. Inside, the casket has a red velvet interior and there is a secret compartment within the lid.

The town of Trapani, on the island of Sicily (which was part of the Kingdom of Naples) was famous for the production of such items, using the red coral in plentiful supply there, and this casket may have been made there or in the region. Very few of these caskets survive.

Maker Unknown (South Italian or Spanish)

A pair of tables, about 1750–70
Both: 89 × 131 × 61 cm

Each of these elaborate console tables has a rare
green-granite top. Their carved decoration is painted
in gold, white, green and pink, and is reminiscent
of the delicate porcelain produced for the court
in Naples at the Capodimonte porcelain factory.
Across the front, in the apron frieze, is the head of
a lion holding two garlands of roses, which wind
their way around all four legs. Placed across the
centre of the leg stretchers is a two-headed swan
with outstretched wings, holding a flower in each of
its beaks. The raised head of one of the two-headed
swans is turned to the left, while the other is turned
to the right. This suggests that the tables were
designed as a pair, since when they are placed
together the swans look across at each other. They
closely resemble decorative furniture in the Spanish
royal palace of El Pardo outside Madrid and may
have been made either in Naples or in Madrid by a
carver who knew the porcelain rooms created in
both cities by Charles III, King of Naples, who
succeeded to the Spanish throne in 1759.

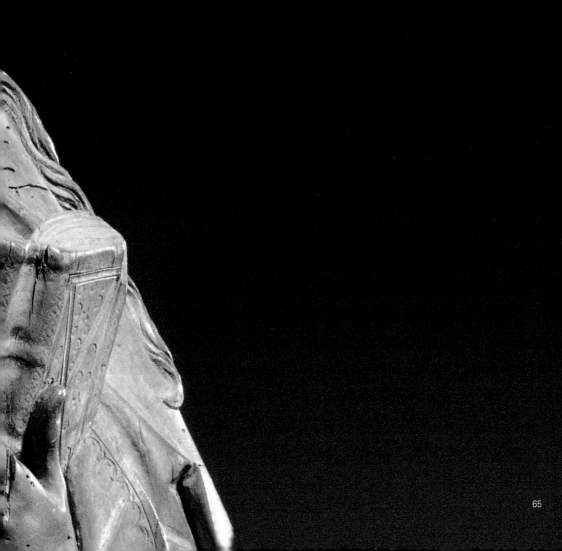

German 1450–1650

The Master of the Polling Altarpiece
(active 1440s)
Saint Peter (left); *Saint Paul*, about 1440
Oil on wood panel, 93.8 × 39.8 cm

The artist derives his name from an altarpiece
painted in 1444 for a convent of Augustinian Canons
in the village of Polling, near Weilheim in Upper
Bavaria. This pair of panels showing Saint Peter and
Saint Paul, set in niches, are the inner wings of an
earlier altarpiece by the same craftsman. Saint Peter
can be identified by his traditional attribute of the
crossed keys of Heaven and the rich vestments that
he wore as the first Bishop of Rome, while Saint
Paul holds the sword with which he was martyred.
The artist produced highly decorative and intricate
surfaces by combining varied architectural motifs,
such as the differently coloured tiles, marble pillars
and Gothic vaulting, with richly patterned clothes
for the figures, in particular those of Saint Peter.
The panels also have a gilded background with
punch decoration.

Previous page: Detail from Tilman Riemenschneider's
A Female Saint, see page 76.

**Workshop of the Master of Frankfurt
(active about 1460–1520)**
The Lamentation over Christ
Oil on panel, 115.3 × 84.8 cm

This painting was produced in the workshop of an
artist known as the Master of Frankfurt, although
he practised in Antwerp. His name derives from
the many commissions he received in the period
1490–1520 from merchants from Frankfurt-upon-
Main in Germany.

The Lamentation took place after Christ had
been taken down from the cross (which can
be seen on Mount Calvary in the background).
Wrapped in a cloth, Christ's body is supported by
Joseph of Arimathea, whilst Nicodemus is by His
feet. The Virgin Mary is supported by St John the
Evangelist as she mourns her son. Behind her stand
the three Maries, among them Mary Magdalene,
carrying the jar of ointment with which she
anointed Christ's feet.

The painting, executed on four wood panels,
was formerly in the collection of the writer,
Roald Dahl.

Maker Unknown (Middle Rhine)

Saint Mary Magdalene, Saint Anne with the infant Mary and the Christ Child and Saint Elizabeth (top); *Saint Apollonia, Saint Dorothy of Cappadocia and an Unidentified Female Saint*, about 1490
Oil on wood panel, 115.5 × 106 cm

These beautiful panels originally formed part of a high altarpiece by an unknown German artist in the church of Bassenheim, near Koblenz. Together with a number of other panels they would have been placed in a frame behind the altar of the church, flanking the centrepiece of a painted or carved Madonna and Child. The first panel shows three married female saints. On the left stands Mary Magdalene carrying the jar of ointment with which she anointed Christ's feet; in the centre is the mother of the Virgin Mary, Saint Anne (with the Virgin Mary as a child and the infant Jesus); to her left is Elizabeth of Hungary, who holds a loaf of bread and a jug of wine as symbols of her work for the sick and poor.

The other panel depicts three unmarried female saints. On the viewer's left is Apollonia, whose teeth were pulled out when she was martyred, which is why she grips an extracted tooth with tongs; in the middle is Dorothy of Cappadocia with the basket of roses which the angel beside her delivered to her tormentor after her death, while on the left is an unidentified female saint carrying the palm of martyrdom.

Maker Unknown (South Germany, probably Ulm)
Noli me tangere (*Christ in the Garden with Mary Magdalene*), about 1500
Painted wood relief, 83.2 × 57.6 cm

In Southern Germany the production of wooden sculpture for religious devotion was widespread. Dating from around 1500, this sculpture was probably part of a much larger altarpiece. Although its back panel and frame are not from the period, the painted relief has retained much of its original character. The title, *Noli me tangere* (Do not touch me) refers to the words the newly resurrected Christ spoke to his devoted follower Mary Magdalene, who was grieving at His tomb. Initially mistaking him for a gardener (Christ is shown holding a spade), Mary suddenly recognised Christ and tried to kiss his robe, which he would not allow. Mary Magdalene can be recognised by the ointment jar (shown below Christ's spade), with which she had anointed his feet just before his death.

Master of the Schwabach Altarpiece
(active 1505–8)
Christ taking Leave of His Mother, dated 1506
Oil and gold on limewood panel, 149.5 × 119 cm

This impressive painting with its lavish gold
background emulates the style of Nuremberg's
most famous painter, Albrecht Dürer (1471–1528).
The main figure group is closely based on a
woodcut print by Dürer of about 1504. The name
of the painter remains unknown, though he is
believed to be the craftsman who painted the
main panels of an altarpiece for the church of Saint
John the Baptist and Martin of Tours in the town
of Schwabach, south of Nuremberg. The patrons
or donors were Michael Lochner von Huttenbach
and his wife Catharina von Plauen, members of
a rich Nuremberg family. Michael and Catharina,
along with their children, also Michael and
Catharina, are depicted as small figures at the
bottom of the painting and are identified by their
coats-of-arms. Michael Lochner the Elder died in
August 1505 and this work, which is dated 1506,
was possibly painted to commemorate him. Over
time, the paint layer has become more transparent,
allowing the underdrawing* to show through.

Tilman Riemenschneider (about 1460–1531)
A Female Saint, about 1515–20
Limewood, 106.7 × 33 × 16.8 cm

Tilman Riemenschneider was one of the most
important sculptors in Germany both before and
during the early period of the Reformation. He
settled in Würzburg in 1483, where for nearly
forty-five years he headed a workshop which
produced numerous altarpieces, statues and reliefs
in materials ranging from alabaster to limewood.
This beautifully carved female saint formed part of
an unknown altarpiece which would undoubtedly
have included other sculptures of saints, among
them possibly a *Saint Catherine* and a *Saint
Elizabeth* which survive in other collections and
have stylistic similarities. This saint's posture
indicates that she probably stood on the left of the
central figure. The sculpture was carved from a
single piece of limewood, which was hollowed out
at the back. Such figures were normally painted,
but Riemenschneider, unusually, often left the
wood of his sculpture bare, allowing the quality
of the carving and of the surface finish to emerge.
He probably never intended that this figure should
be painted. The figure once held an object in her
right hand, which would have identified her, but
this has been lost.

School of Tilman Riemenschneider
Vesperbild or *Pietà*, about 1510–20
Polychrome limewood, 42 × 30 × 15 cm

This small wood sculpture is of the type known
in German as a *Vesperbild*. Such sculpture was
specifically made for religious devotion at the
evening service of Vespers and was intended to
inspire reflection on, and compassion for, the pain
experienced by the Virgin Mary at the suffering and
death of her Son, otherwise known as the *Pietà*.
The back of the statue is uncarved, suggesting
that it was only meant to be viewed from the front.
It appears to be based on a larger sculpture by
Riemenschneider known as the Grosslangheim
Pietà, of about 1490–5. By 1501, Riemenschneider
had a large and successful workshop that employed
up to twelve assistants and pupils at a time.

Attributed to the Circle of the Master I.P.
The Holy Kinship, about 1520
Polychromed limewood 87.5 × 123 cm

This large limewood relief would originally have
formed part of an altarpiece. It represents the family
of Jesus, known as the Holy Kinship, with the infant
Christ in the centre supported by the Virgin's father,
Joachim, flanked on either side by the Virgin and
her mother, Saint Anne. The sculpture has been
attributed to the circle* of the Master I.P. on stylistic
grounds. Although works by him are extremely rare,
the Master I.P. was one of the most versatile and
influential carvers in southern Germany in the
1520s. He and his circle worked in the region of
Passau and Salzburg, and other works by him can
be found in Bohemia. The quality of the carving can
be seen in the intricate folds of the drapery and the
treatment of the hair.

Maker Unknown (Franconian)

Saint Christopher carrying the Infant Christ Child
(front), *Saint Catherine* (back)
Saint George and the Dragon (front) and *Saint Barbara*
(back), about 1519–27, oil on panel
Both: 102 × 40 cm

This pair of double-sided panels once formed
the wings of a now dismembered altarpiece,
the central part of which was probably *The
Lamentation of Christ*, now in the National Gallery of
Scotland. The altarpiece is thought to have
been commissioned to commemorate the death
of Kasimir Friedrich, Margrave of Brandenburg-
Ansbach, who died in 1527. In the *Lamentation* his
coffin is also depicted, surrounded by his family
and peers. Friedrich died while travelling in Hungary,
which may have justified the choice for the front left
panel of Saint Christopher, patron saint of travellers.
The Margrave was succeeded by his brother Georg,
which in turn probably explains the presence in the
front right panel of Saint George. Stylistically, *Saint
Christopher* and *Saint George* are close to the work
of Albrecht Dürer and of his brother, Hans.

On the back are the figures of *Saint Catherine*
and *Saint Barbara*. *Saint Catherine* bears the date
of 1519, some years prior to Kasimir Friedrich's
death, which suggests that these two panels were
originally part of a different altarpiece. They are by
a different hand and were cut down to fit the height
of the *Lamentation*.

Ambrosius Benson (active 1519–50)
Portrait of a Gentleman, about 1525–45
Oil on panel, 37.6 × 29.8 cm

Originally from Lombardy, Ambrosius Benson settled in Bruges in 1518, and in 1519 became a master of the guild of painters. Bruges was then an important artistic centre, and he worked in the studio of the leading Flemish painter, Gerard David (died 1523). He produced mainly religious paintings over the course of his career, but the fine quality of this picture of an unknown man also demonstrates his skill as a portraitist. The sitter's features are individual, and his dress is depicted in great detail, from the fur lining of his cloak adorned with enamelled buttons to the gold pins on his hat and sleeves. He wears much fine jewellery, and is displaying a ring in his right hand. This may be a marriage portrait, in which the sitter offers the ring to his future wife. The painting formerly belonged to the dancer Rudolf Nureyev.

Lucas Cranach the Elder (1472–1553)
Sigmund Kingsfelt, about 1530
Inscribed *Sigmunt.Kingsfelt.Riter*
Oil on panel, 37.5 × 25.6 cm

Lucas Cranach the Elder started his career in Vienna but in 1504 he was summoned to Wittenberg, the capital of Saxony, and appointed court painter by Elector Duke Frederick the Wise. Such was the Duke's esteem for him that he granted him a coat-of-arms, which included the winged serpent that became his monogram (visible on the left of this panel). Cranach remained associated with the court of Saxony for most of his career, producing numerous portraits for successive electors. This picture shows the German *Ritter* or knight Sigmund Kingsfelt. *Ritter* were traditionally professional soldiers who fought in the service of their lords, but by the 1500s they had lost their primary military function and '*Ritter*' was often a largely honorific title. The simple dress and heavy gold chain worn by the present 'knight' suggest an administrator rather than a warrior.

Hans Besser (active 1537–58)

Ludwig, Count Palatine, aged Ten, inscribed
and dated *LUDOVICUS COM/PAL. RHENI. DUX
BAVARIAE ANO./ DNI. 1549. AETATIS. 10*[1]
Oil on paper on wood panel, 59.5 × 45 cm

When this portrait was painted, in 1549, the sitter,
Ludwig (who later became Prince Elector Ludwig
VI), was at the court of Baden. In 1563 he became
ruler of the German principality of the Upper
Palatinate, and in 1576 succeeded to the title of
Elector Palatine. Unlike his father and brother, who
were Calvinists, Ludwig was Lutheran and became
involved in the struggle for dominance between the
Catholic and Protestant doctrines that was then
taking place in the German territories.

Hans Besser painted two similar portraits of
German princes of Baden, Margrave Philibert and
Margrave Christoph II, in the same year. Like them,
Ludwig wears a black cap decorated with gold
petals, an oval hat badge and a number of gold
rings. In addition, a hunting whistle, knife case and
knives hang from his belt.

In 1558 the artist moved from the court of
Elector Frederick II to that of Count Palatine
Ottoheinrich.

1. Ludwig, Count Palatine of the Rhine, Duke of Bavaria, the year
of our lord 1549, aged ten

LVDOVICVS·COM PAL·RHENI·DVX
BAVARIÆ·AÑO· DÑI·1·5·4·9·
ÆTATIS·10

Maker Unknown (German or Netherlandish)
Ewer and basin, about 1580–1600
Silver-gilt
Ewer: 29.2 × 12.7 cm, basin: diameter 53.3 cm

This highly decorated ewer and basin set does not
bear a craftsman or maker's mark and it is therefore
difficult to determine where and when it was
made, though recent examination of the decoration
suggests that it was made in Nuremberg in the late
1500s. The scenes worked into the basin are taken
from the Old Testament and include *Rebecca and
Elijah at the Well* and *The Sacrifice of Isaac*. The
ewer has a beautiful handle in the form of a twisting
dragon. Such expensive and elaborate objects were
made for ceremonial handwashing at important
banquets and would be positioned prominently
on the sideboard or *buffet* when not in use.

Circle of Christian Jorhan the Elder (1727–1804)
Saint John of Nepomuk adoring the Crucifix,
about 1770
Polychrome on oak, 92 × 49 × 21 cm

Saint John of Nepomuk (1345–1393) was a
Canon of Prague Cathedral. He was killed by King
Wenceslaus IV of Bohemia for refusing to reveal
what the Queen had told him in confession.
The king ordered him to be bound and gagged and
thrown into the river from the Charles Bridge in
Prague. This event led him to becoming the patron
saint of bridges and floods. Although Saint John
of Nepomuk was not canonized until 1729, he had
long attracted a cult following.

The small size of the sculpture indicates that it
would have been used for private devotion in the
home. It is carved 'in the round', so that it can
be viewed from all sides, but its relatively
flat back means that it would probably have
fitted into a niche. Stylistically, it is close to
the sculptures produced in the workshop
of Christian Jorhan the Elder in Landshut,
Bavaria. Jorhan was responsible for a
number of altarpieces that survive in
Bavarian churches.

British Portraits

After Hans Holbein the Younger (about 1497–1543)
Henry VIII, about 1560
Oil on panel, 98.2 × 72.5 cm

This imposing picture is a version of the last portrait of Henry VIII (reigned 1509–47) painted by Hans Holbein and his studio, shortly before the artist's death in 1543. Holbein, Henry's court painter, created a series of archetypal portraits of the king that were copied many times and served as an instrument of royal propaganda. In the best-known of these, preserved in a cartoon* in Holbein's own hand in the National Portrait Gallery, Henry's imposing, frontal figure looks down at us in the pose of a heroic knight, hand on his dagger, feet planted apart. The Compton Verney portrait presents a more patriarchal figure, though the king has lost none of his authority and grandeur. Dressed in a lavish surcoat lined with ermine and embroidered with gold thread and precious stones, the king's weighty person is depicted almost full-length, clutching his royal staff and gloves.

The portrait was produced during the early days of the reign of his daughter Elizabeth I (1558–1603), undoubtedly to support the re-establishment of the Protestant branch of the Tudor dynasty after the short rule of the Catholic Queen Mary (1553–58).

Previous page: Detail from portrait of Henry VIII after Hans Holbein the Younger, see opposite.

**Follower of Hans Holbein the Younger
(about 1497–1543)**
*Edward, Prince of Wales, later Edward VI
of England,* about 1542
Oil on panel, 53 × 41.5 cm

Prince Edward, the son of Henry VIII and Jane
Seymour, was born at Hampton Court Palace in
October 1537. His mother died within twelve days
of his birth and the future king was given a separate
household from the age of two. This portrait was
painted when he was five and depicts him not
as a child but as the male heir to the throne. He is
portrayed like his father, frontally, as a large figure
filling the picture's space, his size enhanced by his
costume, a red doublet with gold thread and richly
embroidered slashed sleeves. Like Holbein's
representations of his father, the prince's portrait
is designed to exude power. Edward died, however,
when only twenty years of age. During his short
reign (1547–53) he endeavoured to establish
new Protestant schools. He was succeeded by
his half-sister, the Catholic Mary Tudor. In 1558
Elizabeth I, Edward's younger half-sister, succeeded
to the throne, re-establishing Protestantism in
England. A number of posthumous portraits of
Edward were painted to promote the Protestant
cause, but this one is believed to have been painted
during his lifetime.

Marcus Gheeraerts the Younger (1561/2–1636)
Portrait of a Boy aged Two, inscribed and dated:
Aetatis suae 2 / Ano 1608 (Aged 2, AD 1608)
Oil on panel, 114.3 × 85.7 cm

When this picture was painted it was the custom
to dress young boys in dresses like their sisters
until they were 'breeched' at the age of five or six
to mark their entry into adulthood. The present
sitter, who is only two years old, wears a doublet
and a skirt or 'petticoat' over a farthingale* frame.
A small dagger hangs from his waist near his left
elbow. This was an attribute of the male aristocrat
and distinguishes him from a girl of his own age.
A lace-edged coif and a ruff complement his rich
attire. In his left hand the child holds a bunch of
flowers and a string attached to a robin. Both
flowers, pansies or 'heart's ease', and bird signified
innocence and transience, and hint at the high
rate of infant mortality in this period.

Ætatis suæ 2
Anº 1608

Master of the Countess of Warwick,
(active about 1565)
Sir Thomas Knyvet, about 1565
Oil on panel, 98.9 × 72 cm

Sir Thomas Knyvet was a member of a prominent
East Anglian landowning family. He was knighted
by Queen Elizabeth I during her royal progress*
in Norfolk in 1578, and appointed High Sheriff of
Norfolk the following year. He and his wife Muriel,
who was the daughter of Elizabeth I's Treasurer
of the Household Sir Thomas Parry, lived at
Ashwellthorpe in Norfolk. This fine portrait
noticeably emphasises the sitter's rank, not only
because he wears rich, fashionable clothing, but
also because the porphyry column beside him
introduces noble associations and his pose
expresses ease and courtly elegance.

Maker Unknown (English)
Queen Elizabeth I, about 1590
Oil on panel, 114 × 88 cm

Queen Elizabeth I was painted many times
during the forty-five years of her reign (1558–1603).
She carefully cultivated her image, which was also
circulated through prints and medals, and decreed
in 1596 that all portraits unworthy of her must
be burnt. Elizabeth was most often portrayed as
an icon, the very emblem of monarchy, and her
imagery contained precise references to her
virtues and power. This portrait, painted at the
end of her reign, makes the Virgin Queen appear
much younger than her sixty years, a device which
flatters her but was also intended to underline the
stability of her government. Elizabeth had recently
(in 1588) defeated the Spanish Armada and was
at the height of her power. Her sumptuous and
fashionable bejewelled dress is an external sign of
her magnificence. The crescent moon embroidered
on her bodice alludes to the role she assumed as
Diana or Cynthia, the chaste moon goddess, Queen
of Seas and Lands. Having formerly hung at Brocket
Hall in Hertfordshire, this painting is known as the
Brocket portrait.

**Attributed to Marcus Gheeraerts the Younger
(1561/2–1636)**
*Frances Howard, Duchess of Richmond and Lennox
(1578–1639)*, about 1621
Oil on panel, 57.5 × 44.5 cm

Painted by the most fashionable artist of the
day, this portrait overtly flatters its sitter, Frances
Howard, daughter of Thomas, 1st Viscount Howard
of Bindon. She is presented to the viewer in a
fashionable low-cut bodice, her long hair falling on
her shoulders; light emphasising the translucency
of her beautifully pale skin. Portrayed in this way,
she appears as a prospective bride, and Frances
was a reputed beauty with a côterie of admirers.
However, by the time this portrait was painted, in
about 1621, she may recently have married her third
husband, Ludovick Stuart, as the necklace that she
is wearing, a pendant ornament of a heart and half
moon, was associated with his family. Ludovick was
2nd Duke of Lennox, and then acquired the title
of 1st Duke of Richmond a year before his death.
Frances became known as the 'double duchess'.
She was proud of her rank and wealth, which she
enhanced with each of her marriages.

Jean-Etienne Liotard (1702–1789)
Harriet, Lady Fawkener, about 1760
Pastel on vellum, 73.6 × 58.8 cm

The sitter is believed to be Harriet Churchill, the wife of Sir Everard Fawkener, English ambassador to Istanbul from 1737 to 1746. Fawkener and the Swiss painter Liotard had become acquainted in the Turkish capital, where the artist produced several portraits of members of the British colony. In the mid-1750s the two met again in London, where this portrait was probably painted. Lady Fawkener is described in contemporary accounts as a "very intriguing" and "prettyish" woman who danced well. Here she is shown holding a thread and picking something from a sewing-box, which is perhaps a reference to her husband's former profession as a merchant of cloth and silk. She is set against an unadorned background and portrayed with much directness, two characteristics of Liotard's innovative style of portraiture. The artist specialised in the use of pastel, a soft, chalk-based medium suited both to the detailed depiction of fabrics and to the soft texture of flesh.

Attributed to Daniel Marot (1661–1752)
Table, about 1692
80 × 120 × 70 cm

The design of this unusual table has been
connected with the French-born Dutch artist Daniel
Marot, an architect and designer whose elaborate
creations influenced European court styles of
decoration in the period 1680–1720. Marot left
France in 1685 for Holland, where he worked for
William, Prince of Orange, among other patrons.
During the 'Glorious Revolution' (1688) William,
King James II's nephew, was invited by parliament
to rule England as joint monarch with his wife Mary,
another claimant to the throne of England. Marot
followed them to England and was employed on
the redecoration of the interiors of Hampton Court
Palace. This table is believed to have been made
by William Farnborough for the Water Gallery there,
accomodation intended for Queen Mary's private
use, but demolished by the King in 1700, after her
death. Over its three-hundred-year life, the table
has been repainted a number of times, and in
the 1930s served as a film prop in the studio of
the great Hollywood film-director Cecil B. DeMille.
It has since been restored to its original state
and decoration.

China

Chinese historical periods and dynasties

Neolithic Period: about 4500–about 2000 BC

Shang Dynasty: about 1500–1050 BC

Western Zhou Dynasty: about 1050–771 BC
    Early Western Zhou Dynasty: about 1050–about 950 BC
    Middle Western Zhou: about 950–about 850 BC
    Late Western Zhou: about 850–771 BC

Eastern Zhou Dynasty: 770–221 BC
    Spring and Autumn Period: 770–475 BC
    Warring States Period: 475–221 BC

Qin Dynasty: 221–207 BC

Han Dynasty: 206 BC – 220 AD
    Western Han Dynasty: 206 BC–24 AD

   other Dynasties: 220 – 618 AD

Tang Dynasty: 618–906 AD

Ming Dynasty: 1368–1644 AD

Previous page: Detail from a *lei*, or ritual wine
vessel and cover, see page 125.

China, Neolithic Period

Li (tripod vessel), about 3000–2000 BC
Ceramic, 30.7 cm high

Tripod vessels with bulging legs constitute one of the main categories of Neolithic pottery in ancient China. The bulbous body would have held water or food to be cooked over a flame. Its large surface area would have ensured that heat reached all parts of the food inside the vessel. This kind of pottery vessel inspired many of the bronze vessels used in rituals during the Shang and Zhou dynasties.

China, Late Shang Dynasty

Zun, ritual wine vessel, about 1200–1100 BC
Bronze, 32.5 cm high

This bronze wine vessel is derived, like many other bronze vessels, from a ceramic form. However, the sharp angles of the body and the flanges, difficult to achieve in pottery, emphasise its metallic character. The earlier ceramics on which it is based would have been much more rounded, and would have stood on a low, sloping foot rather than on the taller one seen here. The decoration is extremely fine, with stylised *taotie** faces against a detailed spiral background. This very delicate decoration was possible because the Chinese used a particularly fine sandy clay for the moulds in which these bronzes were cast. It is almost impossible for craftsmen to replicate this degree of detail today.

Inscription on inside base:
Fu (a clan name represented by a utensil for keeping arrows).

China, Late Shang Dynasty

Ding, ritual food vessel, about 1200 BC
Bronze, 24.5 cm high

This tripod vessel, known as a *ding*, was made
for a member of the Shang élite. It is sophisticated
and carefully made. The animal face, *taotie**,
design is clearly rendered and strongly presented
against the background of angular scrolls, which
were later known as *leiwen*,* or 'thunder pattern'.
The *taotie* can also be read as two confronted
dragons, seen in profile, with long, sharply rising
tails. Such ambiguity attracts attention and adds to
the interest of the design. It is not known whether
such complex designs had symbolic meanings.

China, Early Western Zhou Dynasty
Gui, ritual food vessel, about 1000 BC
Bronze, 27 cm wide

This food basin, or *gui*, standing on a high foot with
two handles, was a type that was very widely used
during the Zhou Dynasty, which succeeded the
Shang. The bosses within diamond patterns are
typical of the Shang tradition, as are the fine narrow
handles below the heads at the junction with the
neck. Just below the neck, around the body, is
a band displaying dragons, and similar dragons
decorate the foot.

China, Late Shang Dynasty
Jue, ritual wine vessel, about 1200 BC
Bronze, 23 cm high

Like the *gui*, the *jue* is a very ancient bronze vessel
type. It seems to have formed a pair, or set, with the
gu from at least 1500 BC. By the end of the Shang
Dynasty, when this piece was made, *jue* were
used in large numbers, in groups of five or more in
tombs of the highest élite. The *taotie** faces around
the centre of the bronze are executed in fine scrolls.
Thus the face and its features disappear into the
detailed background pattern. The purpose of the
two posts, one on each side of the lip, is not known,
but possibly they were used for holding the vessel
when lifting it from over a fire.

China, Late Shang Dynasty
You, ritual wine vessel, about 1100 BC
Bronze, 39.2 cm high

The *you* is a standard form of wine vessel, adapted from a simple pottery flask. The twisted bronze handle copies a rope handle of a type that would have been used for pottery versions. The narrow bands of decoration here, as in many other instances, show *taotie** faces executed in fine spirals and quills as an almost abstract pattern. When lifted off the body, the lid would form a vessel in itself, a small saucer standing on a high foot.

Inscription on base and cover:
Fu X zuo fu gui zun yi (Fu [clan name] X [personal name] made Father Gui this ritual vessel).

China, Late Shang or Early Western Zhou dynasty
Fang lei, ritual wine vessel, about 1100–1000 BC
Bronze, 44 cm high

The square *lei,* or *fang lei,* was a bronze version of a very common type of circular pottery vessel, which was, however, made not only in circular form but also in square-section pieces, as here. Indeed these square-section bronzes seem to have been of higher status, because their imposing appearance and sharp angles made it clear to the viewer that they could not be ceramic. Square containers in ceramic would crack at the corners. The roundels on the lid and on the body are typical of this vessel type.

China (Shandong Province), Early Western Zhou Dynasty

Teng hu gui, ritual food vessel, about 1050 BC
Bronze, 23.8 × 32.4 cm high

This food basin, standing on a square pedestal, is one of the most important in the Compton Verney collection. The major food vessels, *gui* and *ding*, were among the most widely used and important vessel types made under the Zhou Dynasty. The square base was also introduced during this period; earlier, the vessels may have stood on stands, but these would have been separately made, possibly in wood. This piece displays elegant birds with long, sweeping, hooked tails and belongs to the second stage of early Zhou casting. Bird decoration was very popular throughout the Western Zhou period.

The vessel is famous for its inscription, which records it as having been made for offerings to the dead and for a relatively high-ranking ancestor. It has been known and documented since at least 1895 and is illustrated in a number of early Chinese catalogues of ancient bronze collections.

Inscription on base of interior:
X hu XX zuo shi huang kao gong ming zhong bao zun yi (XX [personal names] made this precious ritual vessel for his deceased ancestor Duke X).

China, Early Western Zhou Dynasty
Gui, ritual food vessel, about 1000 BC
Bronze, 26 cm wide

This globular vessel, with a neatly fitted lid, demonstrates its close resemblance to a ceramic container in its smooth, almost continuously rounded outline. This vessel type seems to have become widely used around the time of the conquest of the Shang by the Zhou Dynasty. It is one of the many examples of a variety of forms that developed at this time. Here, the *taotie** face is shown in slightly layered relief against the plain background, unlike those of earlier versions, in which angular spirals are used to bring out the definition of the motif. During the Western Zhou Dynasty *gui* vessels (for holding food) became extremely common.

China, Middle Western Zhou Dynasty

Gui, ritual food vessel, about 900 BC
Bronze, 27 cm wide

A *gui* was a vessel for offering food, forming part of a set of vessels. This *gui* is a rare and important piece and has an unusual shape, since *gui* did not originally have feet, but were set on circular or square bases. It was in the second half of the Early Western Zhou and during the Middle Western Zhou period that they appeared cast with feet. The four feet of this vessel end in hooves and the legs are decorated with scales. The looped handles of the vessel bear the characteristic Western Zhou decoration of animal masks. This piece was formerly in the Qing palace collection, and is illustrated in the catalogue commissioned by the Emperor Qianlong (reigned 1736–95 AD).

China, Late Western Zhou Dynasty
Gui, ritual food vessel, about 900–800 BC
Bronze, 36.5 cm high

This substantial covered *gui*, or food basin, is
a form that became widely used following
significant changes in the Late Western Zhou
period. As was normal at this date, the *gui* has a
lid. The deep ribbing pattern copies the grooves
on ceramics of the same date. The vessel bears
a fourteen-character inscription on the base of
the interior, replicated inside the cover. It consists
of a dedication of a rare kind, from a brother to
his sister-in-law. The hope that her descendants
would treasure it forever indicates the high value
placed upon these ritual objects.

Inscription on base of interior:
*Shu xiang fu zuo xin xi zun gui
qi zi sun yong bao yong*
(Brother Xiangfu made this
ritual food basin for his new
sister-in-law. May her
descendants forever treasure
and utilise it).

China, Early Eastern Zhou Dynasty, Spring and Autumn Period

Lei, ritual wine vessel and cover, about 600–500 BC
Bronze, 39.2 cm high

Inscription on shoulder:
Chu shu zhi sun zi huang zhi cong tou (This accompanying container belongs to Zi Huang, the grandson of the *Shu* [rank] of the Chu State).

This vessel is a large container echoing a ceramic form, with a massive lid crowned by an openwork knop. Two large handles carry chains by which the vessel might have been suspended over a fire or carried. Around the body are fine dragon patterns. These surface designs are typical of eastern China, whence this vessel probably came.

China, Late Western Zhou dynasty
Xu, ritual vessel, about 900–800 BC
Bronze, 18.3 cm high

The approximately rectangular vessel is a variant of a form based on the shape of a rounded basin. Its decorative grooves and scale patterns are typical of the Late Western Zhou period. The lid has four flanges, so that, when taken off the basin, it could be inverted to stand as an open tray or shallow dish into which the food from the main basin might be ladled. Lids were very commonly used in this way as an adjunct vessel to the main container, and thus were made in a variety of different forms, depending on the category of food or wine container. The vessel has a long dedicatory inscription inside, mentioning the name of the patron, Jin, and specifying the ritual for which it should be used.

Inscription on base of interior:
Jin shu zuo xiao xu yong lu yong de yong qi mei shou dou fu qi wan nian wei ji (*Jin*, the *Shu* [rank], made this small tureen, to be used at the inspection ritual and to pray for the essence of virtue, longevity and abundant happiness that will last for ten thousand years without end).

China, Western Han Dynasty
Cocoon-shaped Jar, about 100 BC
Ceramic, 30 cm high

This pottery wine-vessel would have substituted
for a bronze container in the tomb of one of the less
high-ranking members of the élite. When members
of the élite could afford it, they buried elaborate
bronze vessels in their tombs, but for many, ceramic
replicas had to take their place. These, however,
were often beautifully painted, as here. In this
example, the red and white decoration recalls not
bronze but lacquer vessels, which at this time were
also high-status objects.

China, Eastern Zhou Dynasty, Warring States Period

Hu, ritual wine vessel, about 500–300 BC
Bronze, 33 cm wide

This *hu* echoes the form of the leather containers carried by the nomadic peoples on China's border, hence its rounded shape and vertical, plain lines. The decoration may also imitate the bindings in twine or strapwork that such containers may have had. The animal faces holding rings, however, are completely Chinese in taste and origin, as is the scroll design between the plain bands. Thus a foreign form has been assimilated and adapted to Chinese tradition.

**China, Eastern Zhou Dynasty, Warring
States Period**
Fang hu, ritual wine vessel, about 350–200 BC
Bronze, 55.3 cm high

This *hu* is a magnificent example of the wine flasks
of the Eastern Zhou period. From about 400 BC
patterns inlaid with silver and precious stones
became common. They were often arranged on the
diagonal, as here, and these designs seem to refer
to the exquisite and often flamboyant textiles that
were made at this time. Indeed, the patterning of
bronze vessels became increasingly diversified as
new skills and technologies came into use. The four
bird finials on the lid, however, recall the very fine
casting of the preceding 'Spring and Autumn' Period
of the Eastern Zhou Dynasty. The large size of the
hu indicates the importance of wine containers in
contemporary ritual.

China, Western Han Dynasty
Zun, wine vessel and cover, about 100 BC
Bronze, 28.5 cm high

During the Han Dynasty, many, if not most, of the earlier ritual vessel types went out of fashion. This circular vessel or *zun,* used for holding wine, took the place of some earlier pieces. It was developed on the model of a lacquer container typical of the southern states of China. The mountain-shaped top reflects the interest of the period in immortals, who were deemed to live in tall, craggy recesses in the high peaks. These mountain shapes are found not only on wine-vessel covers but also as incense burners.

China, Eastern Zhou Dynasty, Warring States Period
Dou, ritual food vessel, about 400–300 BC
Bronze, 23.3 cm high

The *dou*, a vessel on a tall stand with a cover, was one of the dominant forms used in ancient Chinese ritual. In the Late Shang and Early Western Zhou Periods, the *dou* was often made of a high-fired ceramic, perhaps imported from the far south, and indeed these *dou* are among the earliest high-fired vessels known in China. Later on, lacquer versions were particularly common. The *dou* reached the height of its popularity in the Eastern Zhou Period, when it was made in bronze, lacquer or ceramic, depending on the status of the owner and the function of the piece. This bronze *dou* relates very closely in shape to ceramic examples. It is decorated around the middle of the body with a very fine interlaced pattern, which may have been applied through stamping or by making repeated impressions in the casting moulds.

China, Eastern Zhou dynasty, Spring and Autumn Period
Fu, ritual food vessel, about 600–500 BC
Bronze, 34.5 cm wide

The rectangular vessels typical of the late Western Zhou period were given a much more forceful appearance during the succeeding Eastern Zhou period with highly angular shapes. This magnificent example has two equal parts. The upper part or lid could stand beside the lower one, making a pair of offering dishes. Both parts have strong loop handles as well as angular feet. However, the different individuals named in the inscriptions on each part suggest that lid and body may have been matched later. The decoration across the body consists of small repetitive dragon scrolls, giving a very fine texture to the whole surface.

Inscription on inside of cover: *Ni zi xinxhi ren gu* (*Xin*, son of the *Ni* family, owns this food container).
Inscription on base of interior: *Ni zi da zhi ren gu* (*Da*, son of the *Ni* family, owns this food container).

China, Tang Dynasty
Set of twelve painted equestrian figures,
about 700–800 BC
Ceramic, each about 48.5 cm high

These horsemen statues were made to be buried
in a tomb. They would have been placed with a
number of other figures to prepare the deceased
for the afterlife. Each horse is finely modelled with
an expressive head and a long mane, which is
composed of a number of strands of applied clay.
The tail is represented as docked and tied with a
cloth cover. The individual riders are each seated
on a saddle cloth, which is painted as the skin
either of a tiger or of a leopard. They each have
a blanket rolled up behind the saddle and a cloth
of provisions tied around their waist. Riders and
horses are painted with delicate red, white, green
and black pigments.

China, Ming Dynasty
Two Figures, about 1400–1500 AD
Gilt bronze, 112 cm high

The Heavenly Kings, or Guardians of the Four
Quarters, were four in number: the Guardian of
the South (who carried a sword), the Guardian
of the East (who held a four-stringed lute), the
Guardian of the North (who usually carried an
umbrella) and the Guardian of the West (whose
attribute is a snake or pearl). These two surviving
figures from an original set of four are cast in bronze
and gilded. Both wear chain-mail and each stands on
a base cast to resemble a rock. One of them once
held a sword and may be identified as the Guardian
of the South (called *Viudhaka*), while the other
holds a *stupa* (the small pyramid or dome-shaped
Buddhist memorial shrine) and may be a Guardian
of the North (called *Vaisravana*).

China, Ming Dynasty

Tripod incense burner, about 1400–50 AD
Cloisonné enamel on gilt-bronze, 19 cm across
handles

This tripod is very similar in form to early bronze
shapes, such as the Late Shang *ding* in the collection
at Compton Verney. The small roundels just below
the lip recall similar decoration on Early and Middle
Western Zhou bronzes, as do the three legs and
the two handles. However, this piece is made of
brass and decorated with inlaid or *cloisonné* glass.
These inlays form an elaborate lotus scroll, a form
of decoration developed in silverware and ceramics
from about 700 AD onwards. When this piece was
made, the original use of the early bronzes as food
vessels had been forgotten. Such later tripods
commonly featured as the central piece in sets of
five altar-vessels. It held sand, in which stood sticks
of incense. The other four vessels consisted of two
flower vases and two candlesticks.

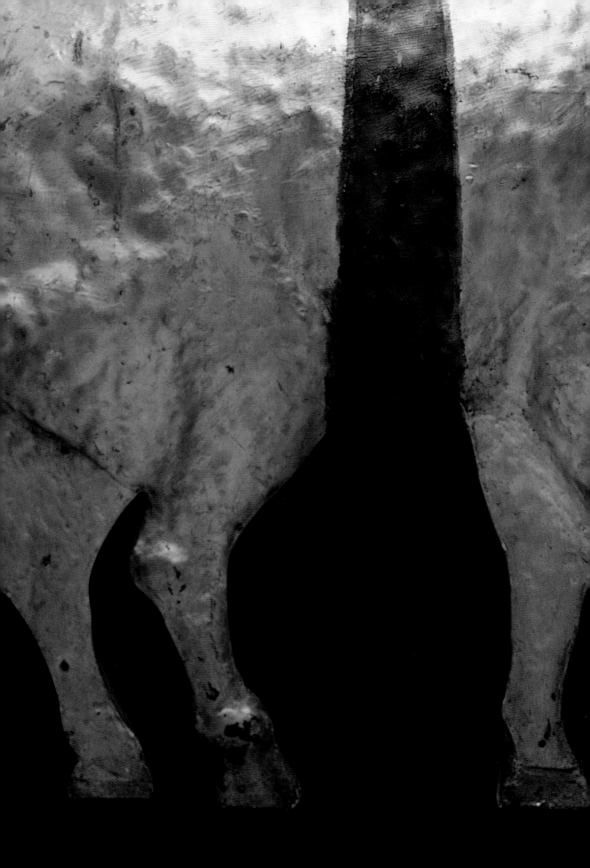

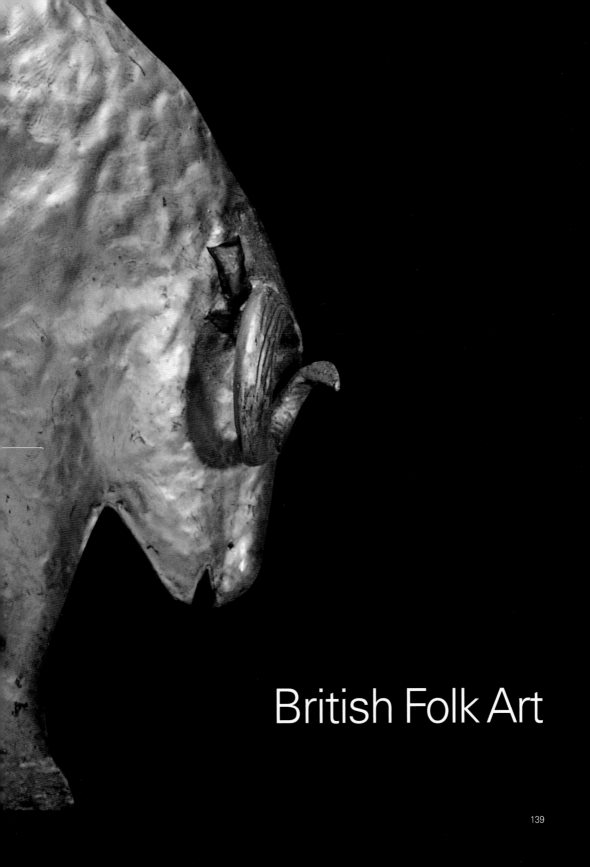

British Folk Art

Attributed to John Collier (1708–1786)
The Dentist, about 1770
Oil on panel, 52 × 74 cm

John Collier, an itinerant schoolmaster also known as 'Tim Bobbin', painted a number of pictures of popular dentistry in connection with engravings for his *Human Passions Delineated*, a book of verse and cartoons satirising English professions, which was published in 1773. In most of these paintings the dentist is shown holding his left leg against the patient's chin, not the right one, as in this work. The engraved version of the scene is entitled *Laughter and Experiment*, with the verse explanation: "A packthread strong he tied in haste/ On tooth that sore did wring:/ He pull'd, the patient follow'd fast,/ Like Towzer in a string.// He miss'd at first, but try'd again,/ Then clapp'd his foot o'th chin;/ He pull'd – the patient roared with pain,/ And hideously did grin."

Previous page: Detail from a trade sign:
The Golden Fleece, see page 155.

Maker Unknown (British)
Country Fête; Country Procession, about 1790
Oil on panel, 62.8 × 77 cm; 61.3 × 77 cm

This pair of paintings presents an idealised view
of a country tradition, the fête in the grounds of
a local well-to-do house. The paintings were
originally joined, as can be seen from the horse,
now bisected, that straddles the composition.
The participants are dressed in their finery and carry
canes and parasols. They arrive on foot, horseback
or in a pony and trap, in an orderly procession.
Welcomed by the host and a lady who carries plates
of food, they can also be seen wandering in the
extensive and finely planted gardens. On the right
of the left-hand picture, near the conservatory,
a man entices the guests with the words:
'Rare Old Port. Strawberries & Cream Ladies'.

Maker Unknown (British)
The Indefatigable, after 1796
Oil on canvas, 56.6 × 76 cm

Many items of folk art were produced by sailors
whiling away their time whilst at sea – including
paintings of ships such as this one. This work shows
the British ship *Indefatigable*, protected by Fame on
the left and Hope on the right, engaging with a French
warship off the French coast in 1796. The caption
ringed in red at the top right reads: *His Majesty's ship/*
Indefatigable of 40 guns/ Sir Edw. Pellew engages
and takes/ La Verginia a French Frigate of/ 44 guns on
the 22nd April 1796 off/ the coast of France Neptune
and/ Amphitrite god and goddess of the/ Seas Riding
Triumphant. Britannia rules the Waves appears in
another caption below. The *Indefatigable* did indeed
give chase to *La Verginia* off the British coast, and
pursued her for fifteen hours, but the contest actually
concluded with the surrender of the British vessel.

Maker Unknown (British)
Daniel Lambert (1770–1809), about 1800
Oil on canvas, 87.5 × 75 cm

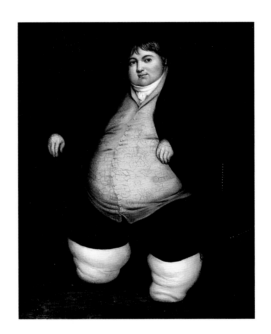

This is one of many portraits of Daniel Lambert, who was a celebrated 'fat man'. Lambert was born in Leicester on 13 March 1770 and died thirty-nine years later in Stamford. As a youth he was a keen sportsman, however, his weight began to increase dramatically and by the age of twenty-three he weighed 32 stone (203 kg). He resigned as Keeper of Leicester Gaol in 1805 when he found that his celebrity as the fattest man on record could be highly lucrative. On his first visit to London he took lodgings at 53, Piccadilly, and 'received' paying visitors between noon and 5 pm. He then made a successful tour of the provinces, drawing large crowds in each town on his route. At his death in 1809, he was said to have weighed 52 stone (330 kg), measuring 5' 11" tall (1.8 m) and 9' 4" (2.84 m) around the waist.

Maker Unknown (British)
Four horn beakers, about 1800
Horn, various sizes – heights 11.8, 10.2, 10, 9.2 cm

These beakers were probably made from a much
larger cylindrical piece of horn, possibly a communal
drinking horn. They were decorated by scratching
a hot needle into the horn. Such vessels were
cheap, light, washable and translucent, enabling
the incised decoration to show up better as the light
passed through them. The better-quality beakers
had thicker bottoms that were pinned into place.
These four beakers are all decorated with similar
scenes, including a coach and horses, fields and
trees, and various buildings, including a manor
house and an inn.

Maker Unknown (Staffordshire)

Two Boxers, about 1815

Both earthenware, coloured and glazed, 22 × 11.5 cm

This pair of painted pottery figures represent prizefighters Thomas Cribb (left) and the American Thomas Molineaux (right), probably made in a Staffordshire factory to commemorate the most famous of their fights, which took place on 28 September 1811 in a field in Wymondham, Leicestershire. Boxing was a popular sport during this period and a considerable amount of money changed hands in bets. This fight was only the second time that these two leading boxers had met, and lasted for eleven rounds. Cribb was the victor, leaving Molineaux with a broken jaw. The fight was also commemorated in a number of engravings.

Maker Unknown (English Provinces)
Girl with Cherries, about 1820
Oil on canvas, 83.4 × 61.8 cm

This endearing portrait shows a little girl wearing a
red coral necklace and holding a bunch of cherries
and a sprig of red flowers. The necklace relates to
the superstition, dating back to antiquity, that coral
warded off evil spirits, and the cherry, symbol of
heaven, was the fruit of paradise. It was common
for parents to commission portraits of their offspring
in a favourite dress, sometimes even after they had
died – infant mortality was extremely high during
this period. In this canvas, the blue dress blends
harmoniously with the background while the red of
the cherries and flowers is echoed in the child's
necklace and booties.

Maker Unknown (Scottish)
An Accident on the Road to Inverness, about 1825
Oil on canvas, 45.5 × 67.5 cm

This dramatic scene of a carriage accident probably
records an actual event that took place on the road
to Inverness. The incident is vividly portrayed: the
smaller vehicle has overturned in the centre of the
road, and the horses in the carriage behind are
trying to break free and have unseated the
coachman. The landscape is painted in sufficient
detail to identify the stretch of road, which was
probably what is now the A96. Castle Stuart is
shown in the background on the left, indicating that
Inverness is to the left of the picture. On the right is
Nairn, and in the distance are ships in the Moray
Firth travelling to Inverness.

George Smart (1775–1846)
Old Man and Donkey, 1833
Collage on paper, 37 × 31 cm

George Smart was a tailor in the village of Frant,
near Tunbridge Wells, in Kent, who made pictures
and figures out of scraps of left-over cloth. His work
was popular and was collected, notably, by Queen
Victoria's uncle, the Duke of Sussex. Smart often
included portraits of local figures in his work, such
as this postman, known as 'Old Bright'. The figure
is made from scraps of fabric pasted onto an
engraving, which the artist has hand-coloured in
watercolour. The picture depicts an actual place:
'Old Bright' is walking down Church Lane in Frant,
towards the post office, which was opposite the
building marked 'Smart's Repository'. On the wall
of this building is a board, where Smart exhibited
his cloth pictures. The artist produced a number of
different versions of this picture, which he sold to
local visitors.

John S. Newton (1828–1854)

Pottergate, Richmond, Yorkshire
Signed and dated *J S Newton 1847*
Oil on canvas, 73.2 × 86.8 cm

Folk paintings frequently depict the places where their makers lived. They were often commissioned by local shopkeepers or businesses keen to see their premises appear in the work as a form of advertisement. This painting of Richmond in Yorkshire shows Pottergate, the main street leading into town. On the left of the painting is 8, Pottergate, a red-brick building with a sign over its front door advertising: 'Newton, Painter, gilder, paper hanger'. The artist's father was also called John Newton. His son was only nineteen when he painted this picture. Local figures animate the view, including Jackie Patterson, cleaner of the local privies, seen on the left with two donkeys. The small man carrying a parcel was Harry Pickall, private postman to the Marquis of Zetland.

Maker Unknown (British)
A Farmer and his Prize Heifer, about 1844
Oil on canvas, 80 × 90 cm

This painting shows Maria, a five-year-old prize heifer bred by farmer Ralph Walker of Middleton Grange, West Hartlepool, County Durham. According to an inscription painted on the back of the canvas, the figure holding the rope is Henry Hamilton, a servant who had been with Ralph Walker's family for over forty years. Maria weighed 154 stone (978 kg) and was slaughtered on 2 April 1844 by Joshua Hodgeson of New Stranton.

In common with many farmers who commissioned paintings of their animals, Walker wanted to commemorate his prize-winning cow before she was slaughtered. The animal is depicted in profile to accentuate the desirable characteristics of her breeding and it is possible that the farmer intended that the artist should exaggerate the animal's size.

Maker Unknown (British)
Nelson, about 1850
Wool and canvas, unframed size 57.6 × 76.9 cm

Admiral Horatio, Lord Nelson (born 1758), was the
great hero of the British Navy who lost his life in
1805 in the Battle of Trafalgar during the Napoleonic
Wars. This colourful stitched wool picture bears
Nelson's name across the centre, and depicts his
flagship, the *Victory*, and his burial monument in St
Paul's Cathedral, London. On the left of this central
scene stands Britannia holding a shield and trident,
with a lion resting at her feet, while on the right is a
sailor with a cannon and a pile of cannonballs.
Carefully executed, the picture was stitched on to
ship's canvas and embellished with applied gold
beading. It is of a type that was made exclusively by
the British Navy and reflects the pride sailors felt for
their ships and the British sea-faring tradition.

Maker Unknown (British)
The Cock Fight, about 1850
Oil on canvas, 76 × 88.5 cm

The cock fight is portrayed at its moment of greatest dramatic tension. Encouraged by the two boys in the foreground, the cocks are beginning to fight. The owners, wearing top hats, eye each other, and each ostentatiously holds a piece of fabric, probably the hood he has just removed from his bird's eyes. The fight takes place in an indoor arena, watched and bet on by a large number of onlookers. At the top right of the canvas, a policeman (a 'Peeler') bursts through the door, brandishing a truncheon. Cock fights became illegal in 1849 and the officer has evidently come to enforce the law.

Maker Unknown (British)
Two Lackeys candleholder, about 1850
Wood, 35 × 18.2 × 93 cm

This carved wooden candleholder depicts two
figures in servants' livery, hands in their pockets,
supporting a candlestick on their shoulders. They are
standing on a small carriage with four rough-hewn
wheels. It is unusual to find a candleholder on
wheels, but this would have been a useful way of
moving a candle around, for example by rolling it up
and down the dinner table at the end of a meal so
that men could light their cigars.

Maker Unknown (British)

Trade sign: The Golden Fleece, between 1850
and 1900
Gilt metal, 36.5 × 68.8 × 24.1 cm

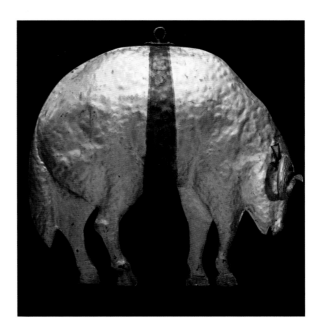

The trade sign was an accessible method of
identifying a tradesman's premises, at a time
when the majority of the population was illiterate.
The Royal Charter granted by Charles I in 1625 gave
the citizens of London the right to erect signs to
identify their trade. Trade signs could be specially
commissioned, but from 1800 onwards they were
increasingly bought ready-made. This sign of a
carved Golden Fleece, made from beaten and
gilded copper, was the traditional sign of a woollen
draper's shop.

Maker Unknown (British)
Military patchwork, between 1854 and 1876
Patchwork, 254.5 × 209.3 cm

This regimental patchwork was made for the Sixth
98th Regiment (indicated by the XCVIII on the Union
Jack flag in the centre and the regiment's colours),
which was later amalgamated with the 64th
Regiment (in 1881) to form the Prince of Wales's
(North Staffordshire) Regiment. The patchwork is
made of various scraps of military material, possibly
taken from old uniforms. The initials *V.R.* (Victoria
Regina) and crown are in the centre of the design,
in honour of the reigning monarch. The two flags
are the regimental colours, below which are stitched
two crossed rifles, a badge that was awarded to
the best 'shot' in the regiment. The patchwork
decoration indicates that the work was made after
1854 (because of the word *Punjaub* on the right-
hand flag, which was authorised from that date
for services in the Punjab in 1848–9) and before
1876 (because after this date the 98th Regiment
had the title 'Prince of Wales's' added to all the
regimental colours).

Maker Unknown (British)
Trade sign: Teapot, between 1850 and 1900
Papier mâché, gilded and painted, 77.7 × 93.8 × 47.2 cm

This giant painted and gilded teapot was made as
a trade sign to advertise either a grocer's or a tea
merchant's shop. Such large signs were traditionally
made to hang or stand outside a shop, whilst
smaller ones might be placed inside the window
or on the counter. As this sign was made of papier
mâché it would probably have been displayed in
the shop, possibly standing on a high shelf. It is
inscribed *Finest Y-Tsien Tea* with the price of tea
(3 shillings per pound) inscribed on the spout. There
are Chinese characters painted on the reverse.

Maker Unknown (British)
Fairground Carousel Pig, about 1850–1900
Cast iron, 79 × 118.5 × 29.5 cm

This cast-iron piebald pig was one of the rides
on a merry-go-round or carousel at a fairground.
Itinerant fairs date back to medieval times and
were a major form of rural amusement, playing a
significant social and economic role in the life of
country communities. As towns grew, fairs became
increasingly busy places of noise and excitement,
and provided entertainment for a largely illiterate
population. With the rise of steam power, merry-
go-rounds became more common and could
include exotic animals and decorated horses
or farm animals such as this one.

Maker Unknown (British)
Weathervane: Seated Dog, about 1880
Iron, 62 × 66 × 5 cm

Weathervanes were significant in an era when rural
and seafaring communities needed to be aware
of the wind direction in order to protect their crops
and ships. The weathervane (deriving from the Old
English 'fana' meaning flag or banner) was also an
expression of the blacksmith's art, usually being
made of beaten iron. Weathervanes could take
many different forms, including those of a cockerel,
swan, dove, fish or ship. Cockerels implied a biblical
reference to Saint Peter, who had three times
denied that he knew Jesus before a cock crowed.

Maker Unknown (British)
Pull-along Bull, about 1900
Wood, 38.5 × 48 × 27.3 cm

This child's pull-along wooden model of a bull on a plank base with four wheels is a very simple home-made toy. The bull's hide is painted in liver-and-white patches and he has a ring through his nose and simple handles for ears. Pull-along or push-along animals on wheels such as this one were very popular in the period before 1900, judging from the number of childrens' portraits in which they appear. Such toys survive relatively rarely because they were cheaply made and suffered at the hands of their young owners.

Maker Unknown (British)
Model of a potter's workshop, about 1900
Wood and metal, 32 × 35 × 24.7 cm

This potter's workshop, probably made by someone who was a potter himself, is an 'automaton' or moving model. The potter and his assistant both move when operated by a key from the reverse. The man on the right turns the flywheel that drives the potter's wheel, and raises his left arm intermittently to mop his brow with a rag. The potter, seated at his wheel, is drawing a pot and, when the wheel turns, his arms move up and down to shape the revolving object. At his side is a pile of clay and on the floor is a tray of unfired pottery ready for the kiln. Behind the two men are shelves of crockery, made of zinc which is painted white.

Maker Unknown (British)
Model of a butcher's shop, about 1900
Painted wood, 37 × 61.5 × 12 cm

This painted wooden model of a butcher's shop was possibly made by a butcher himself. He would have placed such a model in his shop window at night after the meat had been sold or cleared away, and it would have served to show the various cuts and joints of meat available. The figures of the butcher and his boy can be seen standing outside the shop, surrounded by rows of different joints of meat. On the right, a large piece of meat sits on a butcher's block, ready for cutting. Two trees made of grasses stand on either side of the house.

Maker Unknown (British)
Whirligig: A Sailor, about 1910
Wood and metal, 62 × 21.8 cm

Whirligigs were a smaller type of weathervane, found in both town and country. This whirligig, dressed in a naval rating's uniform, is made from painted pine with metal arms that rotate in the wind. The term 'whirligig' comes from 'gig', meaning whipping top, and can be used to describe any spinning or whirling toy. Whirligigs were generally home-made from cheap materials, with articulated elements that moved with the wind. Weathervanes of this type were very vulnerable and unlikely to survive for long in the damp English weather.

Maker Unknown (British)
Whirligig: Pony and Trap, about 1900
Wood with metal parts, 51.8 × 65.5 × 13.2 cm

This whirligig of painted wood and metal
represents two men sitting in a trap drawn by a
horse, the whole mounted with a propeller. The two
figures both wear hats, and one holds the reins of
the horse as it trots beside a tree. Although probably
home-made, it is a sophisticated model. As the
propeller turns, the horse's legs move as if trotting,
and a small hammer located between the feet of
the driver clatters, simulating the noise of the
horse's hooves.

Alfred Wallis (1855–1942)
Schooner approaching Harbour, about 1930
Signed bottom left *Alfred Wallis*
Oil on metal, 32.1 × 41.2 cm

Alfred Wallis spent his life as a fisherman and rag-and-bone man in Cornwall before taking up painting late in life. Untrained, he painted on any surface, including pieces of driftwood. This painting of a schooner with red sails approaching a harbour was painted on a tin tray. It possesses a striking child-like quality. Wallis, who was Cornish, was 'discovered' in 1928 by Christopher Wood and Ben Nicholson, two members of the St Ives artists' 'colony', who were interested in primitive art. Wallis's work has become very popular in recent years.

R. Madison Mitchell (British)
Floating decoy: Swan, 1955
Inscribed on base *R.Madison Mitchell 1955*
Cork and wood, 45.5 × 83 × 27.5 cm

Decoys, which were carvings intended to look
exactly like the birds they portray, have a practical
use for huntsmen. They are made of light materials
as far as possible, so that they can be carried easily.
This elegant swan is made of wood with a cork neck
and head, and a lead keel on the underside, where
it is also signed and dated by its maker.

Elizabeth Allen (1883–1978)

Population Explosion, 1965
Patchwork on canvas, unframed size 38.4 × 47.6 cm

Elizabeth Allen was the daughter of a London tailor who learnt to sew whilst working for her father during World War I. When she retired from her profession of seamstress, moving to a cottage in Sussex, she continued sewing, making collage pictures from rags and odd bits of material. This collage is made from scraps of cloth that include bias binding, brushed nylon, felt, cotton, and *broderie anglaise* (on the bed). Her subjects were chosen from the news and current affairs and frequently offered a serious comment on contemporary religious attitudes and morality. This work was inspired by a report that Allen heard on the radio about a woman who, after taking a fertility drug, had given birth to seven stillborn babies, who appear beside her.

Marx-Lambert collection

Enid Marx (1902–1998)

A Pair of Curtains, about 1950
Linen, 287 × 114.3 cm

The designer Enid Marx made these curtains from
her own woodblock designs. They are made from
untreated linen, printed in black and greenish-
yellow. The design is a primitive, 'jungle'-type
pattern, showing the interest in African sources that
became associated with folk art. It is a large repeat
design reminiscent of zebra stripes or tree grains,
with flowing lines around a central 'eye'.

Enid Marx created a number of designs for
furnishing fabrics throughout her life, but particularly
in her role as Head of the Dress, Textiles and
Ceramics department at Croydon College of Art,
a post she held from 1960 to 1965.

Previous page: Detail from Fantastical
Animal Head, see page 177.

Enid Marx (1902–1998)
A Pair of Curtains, about 1950
Linen, 233.5 × 125.2 cm

This pair of untreated linen curtains was designed
and printed by Enid Marx, who used many of her
designs to decorate her own home. The design has
a black vertical pattern with alternating columns of
oval nut-like shapes and flower-filled cornucopiae.
The cornucopiae are filled alternately with flowers
and wheat or coral and seaweed. They show the
relationship between Marx's work as a designer
and the objects that she collected and displayed
in her home. The cornucopia motif was possibly
inspired by the pair of wall-mounted vases with the
same motif which the artist had in her possession
(see page 174). Enid Marx was an enthusiastic and
prolific textile designer. One of her most famous
fabric designs was the 'shield' pattern used on the
London Underground until the mid-1960s.

Unknown Maker (English)
Wall-mounted vases, about 1890
Pottery, both: 23.5 × 17.2 × 6 cm

This pair of simple, decorative wall-mounted vases
are in the shape of a cornucopia or 'horn of plenty',
a symbol used since classical times to depict peace,
plenty and prosperity. They are decorated with a
delicate green glaze and a moulded oval cartouche *
containing a female figure also holding a cornucopia,
surrounded by acanthus leaves and scrolls. The
designer Enid Marx bought this pair of vases on one
of her visits to antique shops around the country
and used them as inspiration for her design work.
There is a pair of curtains designed by her with
cornucopia motifs in the Compton Verney collection
(see page 173).

Enid Marx (1902–1998)
'Tiger, Tiger', 1958
Linocut and watercolour, 71 × 10.5 cm

Enid Marx also worked as a graphic designer, producing book covers and illustrations. She wrote and illustrated a number of children's books, including *Bulgy, the Barrage Balloon* (1941). This five-colour oval linocut (made by cutting and inking linoleum) by the artist shows a cat in a garden at night and bears the label 'Tiger, Tiger' on its reverse, a reference to William Blake's poem, 'The Tiger', which begins 'Tiger, Tiger, burning bright, in the forests of the night'. The image originated as a design for a large embroidery which was made by some of Marx's embroidery students in Croydon. Enid Marx was extremely fond of her Siamese cats, which accompanied her when she worked in her studio.

Enid Marx (1902–1998)

The letter 'R'
Linocut on paper, unframed size 17.5 × 24.5 cm

Besides her other activities, Enid Marx spent much of her time making woodcuts, engravings and linocuts. She also produced greetings cards, book-plates and labels, for which she was awarded the title of 'Royal Designer for Industry' in 1944. Among her book illustrations for children, she designed an alphabet made up of different animals, which was later printed in *Marco's Animal Alphabet* (2000), and for which this letter 'R' was an original design. The bold and distinctive image of a rhinoceros reflects the simple means of its making, carved out of a piece of linoleum that is then inked. Despite its simplicity, Marx has sensitively depicted the massive wrinkled rhino and its shadow.

Maker Unknown
Fantastical Animal Head
Wood and leather, 23 × 33 × 23 cm

This colourful wooden head of an imaginary animal is typical of the sort of popular and cheaply produced object that caught Enid Marx's eye. The head has a gaping bird's beak in green and tiger stripes on the plumage, with red-ringed eyes. It has a hole on either side and a leather strap which may have been used for hanging. Enid Marx wrote two books on folk art with her friend Margaret Lambert, *English Popular and Traditional Art* (1946) and *English Popular Art* (1951), and was fascinated by the creativity involved in producing such individual objects.

Maker Unknown (Mexico)
Animal model, about 1970
Papier mâché and fabric, 74 × 38 × 27cm

This extraordinary imaginary winged creature has
a crested dragon's head, goat's horns, wings, a tail
and cloven hooves. It has a green shoelace tied
around the middle, which may have been used for
hanging it. Such figures were commonly produced
in Mexico using papier mâché, strips of paper
glued together and moulded in layers. It was
typical of the objects that Enid Marx and Margaret
Lambert collected and with which they were
surrounded in their crowded home. They felt that
they demonstrated the creativity of the untrained
mind, and they provided inspiration for Enid Marx's
book illustrations and other designs.

Maker Unknown (British)
Canal-ware stool, about 1880
Pine, 35.5 × 76 × 26 cm

This long stool in the shape of a bench was made for a canal barge. It is a simple piece of furniture which reflects the friendship that Enid Marx developed with artisans producing objects for canal boats. Marx and Margaret Lambert recorded their interest in English canal barges in their joint book, *English Popular Art* (published in 1951). They found that barges were decorated in a free style that showed gipsy influence, reflecting a true peasant tradition of work. The stool is decorated with castles and flowers, two of the most striking motifs in barge painting. On the top is a romantic scene of a castle with a bridge in the foreground and a lake and mountains in the background, while the trestle-end supports are decorated with floral panels. The sides have colourful lozenge shapes of red, green, yellow, orange and black.

Unknown Maker (English)
Pair of doorstops, about 1850
Cast iron, 32 × 24 × 9.5 cm

This pair of cast-iron Punch and Judy doorstops
was hand-painted by Enid Marx herself after she
had bought them. Mr Punch sits on a pile of books,
holding a pen and paper in one hand and tapping
his nose with the other. He wears a flamboyant
costume, with his mournful dog beside him.
Judy sits on a box holding the baby up to her face.
Mr Punch was a well-known character in folklore
and popular culture, with origins dating back to
about 1300, in the *Commedia dell'Arte* brought by
troupes of actors from Italy to the rest of Europe.
The Italian story-book figure of Pulcinella was
transformed into Puncinello or Mr Punch in England.
Punch was joined by a wife, Judy (originally known
as Joan), and by 1700 the Punch and Judy show
had become an English tradition.

Unknown Maker (English)
Figurehead, about 1850
Carved wood, 124 × 54 × 46 cm

This bold and colourfully painted wooden figurehead is modelled as the smiling figure of a Turkish gentleman, identified as such by his turban, large moustache, green trousers and white and blue robes with a red sash. The long-handled knife tucked into his waistband and his unusual dress lend him a wild appearance, undiminished by the fact that he is holding a book. Oriental figureheads such as this one were among the most characteristic expressions of popular art, particularly in a sea-faring nation such as Britain. They were known on Tudor ships as early as 1500 but gained real popularity only from 1800.

Unknown Maker (English)
Intaglio, 1850s
Glass, 1 × 1.7 × 1.5 cm

This small decorative object is an *intaglio* of clear glass decorated with a design of a cherub scattering flowers and the motto *Il cherche le plus fidèle* (He seeks the most faithful [lover]). The term *intaglio* comes from the Italian for 'carving'; it describes an object in which the design has been hollowed out so that the recessed areas can be filled with ink or sealing wax to impress a pattern. Enid Marx owned several small *intaglios*, which have individual, simple decoration that appealed to her design sense.

Thomas Stevens of Coventry (1828–1888)
The Present Time (A Railway Train), about 1870
Woven ribbon, silk and card, 16.1 × 25.4 cm

This woven picture shows a steam train inscribed *Lord Howe* pulling two railway carriages. It is an example of the fashion for mechanically woven ribbon pictures, known as 'stevengraphs', in the period 1850–1900. Ribbon-weaving in narrow widths on a jacquard loom was a speciality of Coventry, and it was Thomas Stevens's firm there that produced the greatest number of ribbon pictures and the most varied designs. Ribbon-weaving had been an important industry since 1800, when colourful ribbons began to be worn as accessories. By 1850, however, they had gone out of fashion and the industry began to decline. Production of stevengraphs, however, continued, with new subjects often taken from popular contemporary prints in order to appeal to a new market.

Unknown Maker (English)
Stirrup cup, about 1880
Pottery, 10 cm high, 8.2 cm diameter

A 'stirrup cup' was so-called because it was used
by huntsmen when on horseback, in their stirrups,
for a drink before or after the day's hunting. This cup
is decorated with the two faces of the Roman god
Janus, a popular decorative motif. The month of
January is named after the god Janus, who had
two faces and was the god of gates and doors,
thanks to his ability to look in two directions at once.
He could also therefore look back into the old year
and forward into the new one. It seems appropriate
to decorate a cup for the hunt with images of Janus,
as doors and gates need to be opened and shut
across fields during a hunt.

Unknown Maker (English)
Wall plaque, about 1880
Pottery, 21.4 × 19.1 × 2.5 cm

This plaque is pottery modelled to resemble a rectangular picture in a frame. A decorative pink lustre border surrounds a central inscription which reads *Prepare to meet thy God*. It was probably intended for hanging on a wall as it has holes at the top. Each of the three lines of text is decorated with a different pattern and the whole is set in a floral garland, overseen by the all-seeing eye of God. The severe religious text can be associated with the devout religious climate in the period before 1900, when religion was seen as a way of combating the social ills of the age, such as alcoholism.

Appendices

Inscription from interior of *zun* or ritual wine vessel, see page 114.

Glossary

altarpiece Religious painting or sculpture placed above or behind an altar

cartoon Drawing of the same size from which a painting, in particular a wall painting, would be copied, by tracing or other means

cartouche Ornamental tablet with edges in the form of an unrolled parchment scroll, most often framing an inscription or a coat of arms

circle (of an artist) A work resembling, in style, the autograph work of an artist, but apparently not produced by the artist himself but by an imitator, a follower, a rival or an assistant who would know his work well

crozier An archbishop's cross, or the crook or staff of a bishop or abbot

cupola Small domed roof capping a central dome. In Italian cupola designates a monumental dome

dome Circular vaulted roof

de jure By right or law

dormer window From the French *dormir* (to sleep), the window of a bedroom built into the sloping roof of an attic. Dormer windows jut out and are often surmounted by a triangular roof, in which case they are 'gabled'

engraving A technique of printmaking whereby a design is cut into a metal plate (usually steel or copper) with a burin (metal implement). The design is then filled with ink and a print obtained by pressing a sheet of dampened paper over the plate, which is then rolled through a press so that the paper picks up the ink. Multiple prints can be produced from a single plate and are known as 'impressions'

farthingale Framework of hoops to hold a woman's dress extended

fresco Technique of wall painting in which pigments dissolved in water are applied to a wet, freshly laid lime-plaster surface. As the wall dries the colours become permanently bound with it. Fresco is particularly vulnerable to damp, which explains why it has been used mainly in dry countries such as Italy

genre The painting of scenes of everyday life, genre was traditionally regarded as a minor art, by contrast to history painting which portrayed noble actions drawn from celebrated literary sources (traditionally the Bible and classical mythology)

in situ 'On site', in its original location

lapis lazuli Blue mineral, ground by artists from the early Renaissance onwards to produce the beautiful blue pigment known as ultramarine. It came from Afghanistan and was therefore very costly, its application reserved for the most important parts of a painting or illuminated manuscript, such as the blue cloak of the Virgin. It was replaced during the period 1800–1900 by the more affordable synthetic ultramarine

Lateran Obelisk The largest surviving obelisk in the world, originally commissioned by Tuthmosis III for the Karnak Temple in Luxor, Egypt. It was taken to Rome in AD 375 by the son of the Roman Emperor Constantine, Constantius II, and raised at the Circus Maximus, the grand stadium of ancient Rome. It later broke into three pieces and was lost. It was found and re-erected in 1588 by order of Pope Sixtus V, in front of the Church of St John Lateran at the Piazza di San Giovanni in Laterano. A Christian cross was placed at its apex. With the widespread renewal of interest from the 1740s in ancient monuments from classical Greece, Rome and Egypt, obelisks sometimes became used as decorative motifs in Western domestic architecture

leiwen Or thunder pattern, a type of design made up of spirals used in the decoration of Chinese bronze vessels of the Shang and Zhou dynasties. They are thought to represent storms, thunder, rain and fertility

Lesser George With the 'George', one of the constituent parts of the insignia of the Order of the Garter, the order of chivalry created by Edward III in 1348 and the highest military honour that could be obtained. The 'George' is an enamel figure of Saint George on horseback killing the dragon, hanging from an elaborate golden chain, while the 'Lesser George' is a badge of gold enclosing Saint George and the Dragon and worn on a ribbon

naturalistic Depicting the subject with faithfulness, in an unidealised manner

pattern-book Repertory of ornamental and figure designs used as a model or source of inspiration by artists and craftsmen

pendant A companion picture

pictogram, pictograph Sign or character standing for a word, that is at the same time a diagrammatic or debased representation of the thing signified by the word

portico Large porch in the form of a small classical temple entrance, with columns supporting a triangular roof

punched decoration Decoration obtained by imprinting or stamping a design on a material, often used to embellish the gold backgrounds in panel paintings

royal progress Name given to a monarch's journeys around the kingdom, during which he or she stayed at noblemen's houses and was entertained in grand style

taotie Symmetrical pattern consisting of curvilinear lines drawn around a pair of eyes, used principally on Chinese bronze vessels of the Shang and Zhou Dynasties

topographical view View which depicts a natural site, town, buildings or ruins, either with accuracy or with an element of invention.

underdrawing Preliminary sketch on a panel or canvas laying out the composition. Also known as 'underpainting', as on panels the sketch was executed in carbon black superimposed with a thin translucent paint layer, while on canvas it was drawn with a brush. An underdrawing can be fully worked up and establish tones and volumes. In old panel paintings it often shows through, revealing the artist's working method

vault Roof constructed by means of interlinked arches

Vitruvius Britannicus Compilation of engravings of classicising buildings in England in the period 1600–1800, at first compiled and published from 1715 by the Scottish architect Colen Campbell (died 1729). The successive volumes contain plans and sections of palaces, country houses, government offices and churches designed by architects from Inigo Jones to Christopher Wren and Sir John Vanbrugh, Campbell himself and Robert Adam. Together they contributed to the revival of classical architecture in Britain known as Palladianism

woodcut Print obtained by cutting a design in relief on a woodblock. The part of the print which is to be white is gouged away so that when the surface of the woodblock is inked and pressed upon a sheet of paper only the design in relief is printed. Woodcutting is the reverse of engraving

Select bibliography

The House and Grounds

Beard, Geoffrey, *Robert Adam's Country Houses*, Edinburgh, 1981

Bearman, Robert. (Ed.), *Compton Verney: A History of the House and its Owners*, Stratford-upon-Avon, 2000

Country Life Magazine, London, 18 October 1913, pp. 528–35

Dugdale, William, *The Antiquities of Warwickshire*, 2nd edition by W. Thomas, 2 volumes, London, 1730

Girouard, Mark, *Life in the English Country House*, London, 1978

Harris, Eileen, *The Genius of Robert Adam – His Interiors*, London and New Haven, 2001

Tyack, Geoffrey, *Warwickshire Country Houses*, Chichester, 1994

Verney, Richard Greville, 19th Baron Willoughby de Broke, *The Passing Years*, London, 1924

Naples 1600–1800

Art in Italy: 1600–1700, exhibition catalogue, Detroit Institute of Fine Arts, Michigan, 1966

The Golden Age of Naples: Art and Civilization under the Bourbons, 1734–1805, exhibition catalogue, Detroit Institute of Fine Arts, Michigan, 1981, 2 vols.

Martorelli, Luisa and R. Muzii, *In the Shadow of Vesuvius: Views of Naples from Baroque to Romanticism, 1630–1830*, exhibition catalogue, Accademia Italiana delle Arti e delle Arti Applicate, London, 1990

Percy, Ann, *Bernardo Cavallino of Naples: 1616–1656*, exhibition catalogue, Cleveland, Ohio, 1994/5

Salerno, Luigi, *New Studies in Italian Still Life Painting*, 1989

Spike, John T., *Italian Still Life Paintings from Three Centuries*, exhibition catalogue, National Academy of Design, New York, 1983

Whitfield, Clovis and Jane Martineau (Eds.), *Painting in Naples, 1606–1705: From Caravaggio to Giordano*, exhibition catalogue, Royal Academy of Arts, London, 1982

German 1450–1650

Tilman Riemenschneider: Master Sculptor of the Late Middle Ages, a catalogue of an exhibition held at the National Gallery of Art, Washington DC, and the Metropolitan Museum of Art, New York, 1999.

Baxandall, Michael, *The Limewood Sculptors of Renaissance Germany*, New Haven and London, 1980

Jopek, Norbert, *German Sculpture, 1430–1540: a catalogue of the collection in the Victoria and Albert Museum*, London, 2002

Kahsnitz, Rainer and William D. Wixom, *Gothic and Renaissance Art in Nuremberg 1300–1550*, Metropolitan Museum of Art, New York, 1986

Mueller, Theodor, *Sculpture in the Netherlands, Germany, France and Spain 1400–1500*, Harmondsworth, 1966

Osten, Gert Von der and Horst Vey, *Painting and Sculpture in Germany and the Netherlands 1500–1600*, Harmondsworth, 1969

Stepanov, Alexander, *Lucas Cranach the Elder, 1472–1553*, Bournemouth, 1997

British Portraits

Brooke, Xanthe and David Crombie, *Henry VIII Revealed: Holbein's Portrait and its Legacy*, London, 2003

Hearn, Karen (Ed.), *Dynasties: Painting in Tudor and Jacobean England 1530–1630*, exhibition catalogue, Tate Gallery, 1995

Strong, Roy C., *The English Icon*, London, 1969

Strong, Roy C., *The Elizabethan Image: Painting in England, 1540–1620*, exhibition catalogue, Tate Gallery, London, 1969

Strong, Roy C., *The Portraits of Queen Elizabeth*, London, 1987

Strong, Roy C., *Tudor and Jacobean Portraiture*, exhibition catalogue, National Gallery of Washington, Washington DC, 1990

China

Clunas, Craig, *Art in China*, Oxford, 1997

Rawson, Jessica, *Chinese Bronzes, Art and Ritual*, exhibition catalogue, British Museum, 1987

Rawson, Jessica (Ed.), *Mysteries of Ancient China: New Discoveries from the Early Dynasties*, London, 1996

Whitfield, Roderick (Ed.), 'The problem of meaning in early Chinese ritual bronzes', *Colloquies on Art & Archaeology in Asia* No.15, Percival David Foundation of Chinese Art, School of Oriental and African Studies, University of London, 1990

Yang, Xiaoneng (Ed.), *The Golden Age of Chinese Archaeology: Celebrated Discoveries from the People's Republic of China*, exhibition catalogue, National Gallery of Art, Washington, 2000

British Folk Art and Marx-Lambert collection

Ayres, James, *Two Hundred Years of English Naïve Art 1700–1900*, Virginia Art Services International Touring Exhibition, Alexandria, Virginia, 1996

Ayres, James and Andras Kalman, *English Naïve Painting, 1750–1900*, London, 2nd edition 1980

Lambert, Margaret and Enid Marx, *English Popular Art*, London, 1951, 2nd edition 1989

Wortley, Laura, *Everyday Images. Naïve Painting of Daily Life, 1750–1900*, exhibition catalogue, River & Rowing Museum, Henley-on-Thames, 2003

Young, Robert, *Folk Art*, London, 1999

Photo credits